Easter Laggan

FIT FOR
CYCLING

Les Woodland

Foreword by Sean Kelly

PAVILION
MICHAEL JOSEPH

Published in association with The Sports Council

Acknowledgements

I would like to thank all those who have helped me with this book, especially Sean Kelly and Professor Clyde Williams.

First published in Great Britain in 1988 by
PAVILION BOOKS LIMITED
196 Shaftesbury Avenue, London WC2H 8JL
in association with Michael Joseph Limited
27 Wrights Lane, London W8 5TZ

British Library Cataloguing in Publication Data

    Woodland, Les
      Fit for cycling. – (Fit for).
      1. Cycling
      I. Title
      796.6   GV1041

    ISBN 1-85145-257-5

Printed in Spain by Graficas Reunidas, Madrid

CONTENTS

Sean Kelly is one of the fastest road race sprinters in the world and is unusual in also being a good all-rounder. His total professional wins are in excess of 150 and has won 10 of the world's major classics, including the formidable Paris-Roubaix with its 100 miles of cobbles. He was three times Super Prestige Pernod Champion, has been unofficial world champion on the FICP/VELD computer rankings for the past four years, has won five stages of the Tour de France and has won the Paris-Nice for the last six years – an unbeaten record.

FOREWORD

The other day, I was at the end of a big race. The television was there; there were crowds of people, and noise, and team cars and people asking for signatures and reporters wanting interviews.

That's the way it is for a professional on the Continent.

But then I suddenly remembered back in Ireland, when I was just a boy from a farm, a kid with a bike riding his first race with nobody but a few friends and club-mates to come and watch.

The point is that everybody starts off that way – just another unknown.

After that, two things sort out who's going to be a champion, who's still going to be racing along farm roads with just clubmates and stray dogs to watch them. The first is a little bit of pre-selection, a healthy heart, a shrewd brain, and arms, legs and everything else all in the right places.

But after that, it's just determination. I've seen champion bike riders, men who are heroes all over Europe, with their eyes watering from the pain that bike racing's putting them through.

If you can do that, if you train properly, if you can learn by your mistakes and you're humble enough to learn from others, you'll improve beyond your imagination.

Read this book and see what it does for you. But for my sake, don't get too good at it – life as a professional's plenty tough enough already!

Good luck.

Sean Kelly

1 IN THE BEGINNING . . .

I used to be a swimmer once, a long time ago. It has to be a long time ago because you're over the top at 15, when you're a swimmer. Anyway, all I had to do was turn up with a towel and my swimming trunks, swim a handful of races, and then catch the bus home again. I was a backstroker, so I didn't even have to dive.

Heaven knows why I became a cyclist, because nothing could be more complicated by comparison. Suddenly 15 was very young. And apart from time trials, which like swimming had a refreshing consistency, the races were any distance that the organizers chose, uphill and down, morning or afternoon . . . anything.

And that's the problem with writing training books, because bikies are as varied as the events they ride. Yet luckily there is a common theme – you. Look at yourself before you start riding. Have you been cycling for some years, or are you new to the game or making a comeback? Are you fat or thin, employed or unemployed, slender or heavily built? Do you smoke? How old are you?

I ask these questions because you don't want to do yourself a mischief. You won't hurt yourself on a bike as you might in running; you certainly won't drown as you could in swimming. You're not subjected to violent muscular strains, but you *are* held up and kept going by the wheels that perform as powerful gyroscopes. That means it's easy to carry on riding beyond any sensible limit. Exhausted joggers flop out; knackered hockey players can't hit the ball straight or at all. But on a bike the motion is smooth and your weight is supported. You don't fall over so, quite literally, you can go too far.

You can also press your heart rate quite high – there'll be a lot of talk about that. And although exercise won't damage a healthy heart, violent effort can be a risk to

1

unhealthy ones. You can no more strain a dicky heart without looking for trouble than you can safely drive an old banger flat out down a motorway. Something, some time, will give.

Now, I'm just an ordinary bloke. I don't want all the expense of solicitors just because you've followed my advice and done yourself harm. So if you've any reason to suspect heart trouble, or if you've been inactive for a number of years, or if you're over 35 and starting on your bike without several years of playing strenuous games – check first. Ask your doctor's advice.

I assume all through this book that you've ridden before. An old professional team manager called Roy Thame told me once that you had to be fit enough to start training. He's dead right. You'd no more start thrashing around on your bike without a build-up than you'd run flat out without a fair bit of jogging as preparation. The minimum starting point must be to ride 45 miles in three hours.

If you haven't got that far – and not many people could when they started – you don't really need to start training yet in any formal sense: just ride your bike as often as you can. You might like to go straight to the chapter on the bike itself, to make sure you're sitting properly. Most beginners are so badly positioned on the bike that they're wasting as much effort as they're getting through to the wheels.

Just ride your bike as often and, within reason, as far as you can. Get to enjoy the very feel of cycling. Learn to love the fresh air, the little lanes (you might want to use busier roads for training, but use the quietest of lanes for simple enjoyment) and the feeling of freedom. Above all, learn to feel at home on your bike because you're going to spend many hours on it in the future.

Who Makes a Bike Rider?
There are no age limits – you can ride as young or old as you wish. You can be tall or tiny. There are no rules. Obviously it is rare to find anyone younger than 12, for example, riding competitively. But riders of 14 and 15 are old enough to have their own age category, and it's by no means unusual to find 65-year-olds in veterans' (over-40) events. Some of the most prominent names of the past twenty years, like

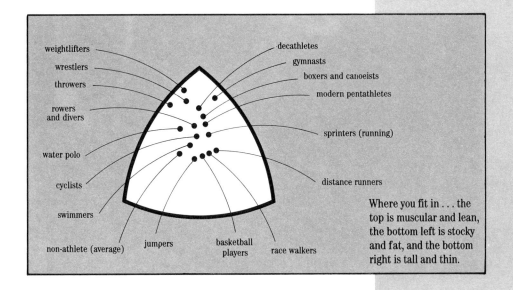

weightlifters

wrestlers

throwers

rowers
and divers

water polo

cyclists

swimmers

non-athlete (average)   jumpers   basketball
players   race walkers

decathletes

gymnasts

boxers and canoeists

modern pentathletes

sprinters (running)

distance runners

Where you fit in . . . the
top is muscular and lean,
the bottom left is stocky
and fat, and the bottom
right is tall and thin.

Joop Zoetemelk and Raymond Poulidor, were still at the top in their forties. The
Belgian, Eddy Merckx, was 19 when he became world amateur road race champion.

There are tall thin riders and short stocky ones, and they do well, but it's
remarkable how the best in the world so often fit into a tight range. The Olympic
records show how on the whole boxers, canoeists, gymnasts and decathletes are
more muscular than cyclists; swimmers, distance runners, race walkers and
basketball players are thinner and more lightly muscled (see above).

Typical Olympic cyclists are just less than 5ft 9in – about the average for the
population as a whole – smaller than short-distance runners like sprinters (average
6ft), middle and long-distance runners and many other sports. They have less body
fat than almost all other athletes, and they weigh 151.2lbs. And then, just as you
think you've found the formula for the perfect bikie, someone comes along and ruins
your formula. You've only got to look at the different shapes and sizes in a
professional team, or at the annual time-trialists' national prizegiving, to see that
there's more to it than size and weight.

Probably the biggest problem that we've faced in Britain for many years is that
cycling has been an unknown sport. Kids have always had bikes, but not until the

rise of televised cycling during the 1980s has racing been considered a worthwhile choice for youngsters. Even now it's a pretty costly sport, both in equipment and in transport to distant races. And it's also pretty tough.

The former professional champion and Milk Race winner, Les West, said once: 'Cycling's problem is that it's never been the first choice of physical education teachers. Any kid that shows aptitude for sport gets directed into football or athletics or something, and never into cycling. Cycling ends up with all the oddballs who wouldn't fit in, weren't good enough, or whatever.'

West himself had to make a choice between professional football and amateur cycling. He chose cycling. So, as a youngster during West's glory days, did an Irishman called Stephen Roche. The change in cycling and in schools had spawned the English Schools Cycling Association which, with the higher cycling authorities turning a blind eye, runs an international boys' race each spring. Tucked away on the early start sheets of the Esca Internationals have been many who've made decent names for themselves later. Among them was Stephen Roche, who won the Tour de France and world championship in 1987.

So, your age doesn't really matter, provided you can ride a bike and you're healthy. Roche and I were both unknown, rank outsiders once. The difference was that those who can, do, and those who can't, write books!

Track sprinters tend to be shorter and more heavily built, sometimes with surplus fat. Roadmen are leaner but muscular; natural climbers like Robert Millar are lean and light but with muscle power disproportionate to their weight.

New fabrics mean these skin shorts are snugger, lighter (and more expensive, although the rule is to buy the best you can afford). Incidentally, always wear two layers at least on your upper body in case you fall off. Two layers will slide and protect you; one layer will wear through and hack you to shreds.

Bib shorts are a variation. They give better protection to the small of the back and there's less chance of a sweat band to get cold.

Once you could buy unperforated racing shoes for winter, even fur-lined shoes. Some shops might still stock them, but increasingly popular now are overshoes, which have a hole cut in the sole for shoeplates.

Cycling shoes have light, perforated or net uppers and heavy, rigid soles. Most shoes have shoeplates on the soles to grip the pedals, but several manufacturers now make combinations of pedals and shoes which fasten together without conventional clips, or straps.
But remember that the system hasn't been perfected; at least one professional has lost a Tour de France stage because his patent binding failed at the last moment.

2 INSIDE INFORMATION

You're a complex machine that runs on simple principles. If I explain them, it will make it easier to understand your training.

Basically, your muscles are collections of little electrical motors. Electricity runs down nerves and triggers off a reaction with the sugar and oxygen brought in by your blood. The reaction makes the muscle fibres shorten, the muscle jerks and a limb moves. It's as simple as that.

Provided you don't do anything strenuous, that simple routine will carry on from the day you're born until the day you die. You don't even have to think about it. You're getting enough oxygen and fuel into the muscles and the exercise is described as *aerobic*.

The problem comes when you ask more of yourself. That's when you realize you're not as fit as you thought, and that's how you lose races. Suddenly you can't get enough oxygen into your blood because the lungs aren't very good at it. The muscles get blocked because they're producing waste faster than they can get rid of it. Then acids build up, which make the muscles hurt, and you're forced to slow down because you can't cope any more. You've built up an oxygen debt, or gone into *anaerobia*.

The more exercise you take, the more blood vessels you'll open through your muscles and the more endurance – *local muscular endurance* – they'll have. They'll work longer and harder before they ache. At the same time, your lungs open more air sacs with which to transfer oxygen to the blood – *oxygen uptake*. Your heart will grow larger to hold more blood, so it can pump out more with each stroke before reaching its maximum speed (*stroke volume*). Your brain will learn the fine muscles will learn to use more fibre bundles at a time and increase your push (*strength*). What happens beyond this stage is rather more complicated, so we'll come to it later.

Endurance

Endurance is exactly what you think it is – the stamina to keep on going. It makes no difference whether it's a 4,000m pursuit, a 24-hour time trial, or the Tour de France: if it's a matter of endurance to you, that's what we're talking about.

The greater the distance, the greater the endurance demanded. That's because speed and the chances of oxygen debt are both reduced. As you'll see from the table below, drawn up by the American sports doctor Ed Burke, endurance is pretty important. Only in the highly specialized events of the kilometre and individual sprinting – races that no beginner would tackle – does endurance count for less than

Event	Time of race	Flat out	Speed	Cruising
100m road race	3hrs55 – 4hrs	0%	5%	95%
100km criterium	2hrs05 – 2hrs15	5%	10%	85%
100km team TT	2hrs10 – 2hrs20	0%	15%	85%
25m time trial	52mins – 1hr	0%	10%	90%
25m criterium	50mins – 1hr	5%	15%	80%
10m track	20mins – 25mins	10%	20%	70%
4km individual pursuit	4mins45 – 5mins05	20%	55%	25%
Kilometre sprint	1min07 – 1min13	80%	15%	5%
Match sprint	11secs – 13secs	98%	2%	0%

25 per cent of time. All the non-specialist events rate 70 per cent or more.

At one time, cyclists did nothing but endurance training, and even then they did it pretty badly. The standard way was to clock up miles. The more done at one go, the better. Miles maketh the man.

Bill James, a coach who raced in the 1930s, once said: 'I wince when I think of some of the get-fit ideas I followed as a teenager. One such bash stands out in my mind – the annual Corfe Castle run. There and back in the same day, 230 miles and all on a fixed wheel, of course.

'The last 30 miles or so were virtually done in an insensitive daze, but since the big boys – Fleming, Walters, Burgess, Pond, Hill – did this, you didn't question why.'

Or as Greg LeMond says: 'When I first started to race, I thought training meant simply riding hard until you got in shape. To me it seemed that if you didn't feel pain, you weren't getting any benefit. After a short while, I discovered that I wasn't getting in shape, only getting tired after my training rides . . . A systematic approach to training is one of the key factors in becoming a successful cyclist.'

What never occurs to many riders is that speed drops with distance, so that progressive pressure on the body (the *overload effect*) is replaced mainly by fatigue, as LeMond realized. You *will* get faster by riding endless miles, but the improvement is solely by chance and it's also very exhausting. There's no point in any training that builds such fatigue that you're not ready to train again at your next

Always dress warmly for training; don't train in shorts unless it's a hot summer's day. Always make sure the small of your back is well covered and your chest protected, it might not give you the speed of Sean Kelly and Stephen Roche, but it won't land you in bed either.

Even the racing season doesn't guarantee good weather: dress accordingly.

session or, worse, that leaves you less than daisy-fresh for competition. In fact, most riders who concentrate on distance training go faster only because the weather picks up during the season and because their skill is improving, particularly in pace judging.

It follows, therefore, that improvement comes by riding at your limit. So, if you want to improve your aerobic ability, the way your body will supply sugar and oxygen and get rid of the waste, you have to ride constantly to the edge of oxygen debt – but no further. If you go into oxygen debt, you'll have to slow down a bit to recover, and that defeats the purpose. It'll have another, beneficial effect, but not the one that you want at the moment.

Riding fast cruising miles as if you were riding a time trial (90 per cent cruising, remember) is known as *steady state* training. Your body is in a steady state of supplying and getting rid of its fuel. The trouble is that it's not a very good phrase, because the word steady is misleading. It suggests an easy ride. It shouldn't be. As the junior coach, Les Jordan, observed: 'Too many people concentrate on the steady rather than getting into a state.'

Overload Effect

Like any training method, steady state makes you fitter because your body responds to being taken to its limit – either in endurance or speed or strength or skill. It's constantly assessing what it is you want of it and preparing to cope. Here's an example: if you break your arm, the bone will grow thicker and stronger at the point of the break. It's as if your body has worked out that it will get a pretty severe whack there again some time and it doesn't want to be caught napping again.

The longer you keep at your limit, the more you will improve. But remember that the more you improve, the more you've extended your limits, so the harder you have to train. There's no point in repeatedly training over the same distance in the same time because there's no progression, no overload and therefore no improvement.

Elementary Steady State

The most basic steady state training is merely exposure to your bike. If you haven't kept up your training all winter, start by riding at up to a quarter further than your mid-season distances. You'll have to use some discretion here if you're aiming for 12 or 24-hour time trials, of course. In fact, the probable maximum would be 110 miles for seniors, 70 miles for juniors, 40 miles for schoolboys.

Try to ride long distances non-stop if you can. If you can't, limit yourself to just one break. Certainly anything less than 60 miles should be non-stop.

If you've been riding all winter, this stage probably won't be necessary anyway, so you can go straight on to basic training.

Basic Training

The fundamental rule is that proper training (by which I exclude the elementary steady state) has to be faster than race speed. Now if you train at the race distance or further, you'll ride at your race speed or slower. That's logic. At times, by chance, your training might be harder or faster than your races, but the percentage of useful exposure is minute compared to the period of fatigue. The trick is to reduce your training distance a little and then split it into sections. You can then maintain the

10

distance but vary the sections to increase your output. In that way you make your training progressive and keep up the overload. Anything less is a waste of your time.

Start by cutting a quarter off your mid-season race distance. If that's 50 miles, the result will be 38 miles (don't worry about odd fractions). If you want to concentrate on 100-mile road races or time trials, it'll be 75 miles, and so on.

Now divide the result by four. I'll concentrate on the 50-milers, but the arithmetic's the same for all distances. A quarter of 38 is about nine miles, so that's the length of training route that you need to find. Choose one that's as flat as you can manage in the area that you live – certainly avoid any hills that'll put you deeply into oxygen debt. You could find one nine-mile circuit or use a shorter one more than once; it doesn't matter which, provided it's not too mountainous.

Start with a warm-up and then go straight into your nine miles, riding them as though they were a national championship. Use a gear a little lower than you would in the race. Keep the effort on all the time – you're not gaining anything unless you're right on the edge of oxygen debt – but don't take yourself into oxygen debt deliberately by sprinting out of corners, chasing mopeds or tackling hard hills. Going into oxygen debt has other benefits, but not the ones you want at the moment. Nor is this the best way of achieving those benefits.

Ease up the moment the nine miles are over, change into a low gear, and pedal slowly with your hands on the tops until your breathing's entirely back to normal. Then ride the next nine miles as fast as you can, and repeat the process until you've done all four legs. And then you ride home.

This is aerobic training, so it's primarily a breathing and endurance exercise. That's why you leave a long enough gap between the hard legs to let your breathing recover. Some oxygen debt is inevitable with any exercise, but there's no point in starting a session with it. That'll only make the session less useful.

And Then . . .
After three sessions of 38 miles, maintain the total training distance but now divide it into eight legs. That keeps the progression and overload. It means you can ride

faster. But you *must* keep the full recovery period between each hard stretch. It's better to have too long a recovery than too short; it will be the other way round later on, so make the most of it.

Finally, after another three sessions, keep the total distance but split it into 16. Now you can really ride hard, but don't sprint. It's top-rate cruising that you're aiming for, the kind of consistent output that burns off the opposition. Later, in more advanced training, you'll be getting to handle the absence of recovery periods and the onset of oxygen debt, but that's all to come. That will all be built on to this foundation of endurance.

But There's More . . .

It may be helpful to know exactly which elements play the greatest parts in the various kinds of bike racing. Norman Sheil, who used to be the national coach, divided them up as shown in the table below, where 1 stands for strength, 2 for speed, 3 for stamina and 4 for skill.

| Sprint | 12-hour | Hill climb | | 25 miles | Road racing |
		short	long		
1	3	1	1	4	All, in any
2	1	4	4	1	order
4	4	2	3	2	
3	2	3	2	3	

Skill – the ability to do something precisely, with a minimum of wasted effort – might figure higher than you expected. According to Sheil, a former world champion pursuiter, national time trial champion and Tour de France rider, it *could* be top in road racing and definitely *is* top in 25-mile time trialling. If his table had extended to cyclo-cross, I've no doubt it would have been pretty near the top in that as well.

In road and cyclo-cross it's pretty obvious that the skills of bike handling, cornering, hill-climbing, tactics and simple balance all figure prominently.

In time trialling the prime skill is judging your pace accurately, so that you don't either finish with surplus energy or blow up badly five miles from home. You get this judgement from riding set distances all-out, which is what the training I've specified so far will achieve. Your early races, which I suggest should be rides that don't matter other than for training, will give you a lot of the rest.

But although you can stand at a cyclo-cross and marvel at the show of bike handling, quite the opposite is the case at a time trial. It's often a great display of bobbing bodies, bikes zig-zagging gently to the effort of pedalling, along with projecting knees and a host of other faults. Many of the best riders have got their skills honed to a silky smoothness – and I suspect that as much as anything is what makes them go that much faster – but from time to time you can stand on a roundabout and watch the best go round as though they had pitted headsets.

Now, for a short while I agreed with those coaches who said riders should always train alone. That way you got your own maximum, whereas riding in a group brought you only an average. The logic remains immaculate, but it overlooks the fact that most skills come best in a group, that mass bashes break the monotony of solitary training, that they're enormous fun, and that they're a simple if not entirely reliable way of seeing how fit you are compared with your companions.

I'd say that about a third of your training sessions should be in a group, whether you're a road rider or a time trialist. The other training benefits are haphazard, but they exist, and group riding is the only way you'll get them all.

The bashes I knew best were on great loops of 35 miles, out from west London, through Slough ('Caution, safety town' the signs used to say as we hammered through) and on round the back of Heathrow airport. The trouble was that the roads were occasionally dangerous and we probably made them more so; the weakest riders were shot off by half distance and left to ride home miserably by themselves; the best riders weren't being drawn out enough; and 75 per cent of the bunch were holding themselves back slightly to figure in the final sprint.

Much better, surely, to use a smaller circuit. If you find a loop of just four or five miles, it has many benefits: you can do a U-turn and meet the bunch coming the other way if you puncture or get dropped; you can ride fewer or extra laps to suit your own needs; you can set intermediate objectives, like village signs or end-of-lap sprints, rather than concentrate on the final gallop; you can attack and take chances knowing that all is not lost if you blow up badly; you can find a course without traffic lights and dangerous junctions; you can run your bashes as a handicap more successfully if the course is shorter and the numbers not too great. Also, there are more corners on repeated short circuits, and you don't find yourself having to hold back because you're not sure of the way.

How Often?

There'll be more on how to work out a training schedule later in the book, but remember this: most sports physiologists reckon there's no point in training fewer than three times a week. Or, rather, that you won't get the full benefit, because obviously all exercise is valuable.

Now, that takes up a lot of time, another good reason for training as economically as you can. You don't *have* to train that often. It might be that you just can't. The greatest reason for giving up racing is the time needed for a career, to get married, to set up a home. Some riders make a comeback later in life because they've done all those things and once again have the time; others get inspired because the enthusiasm they gave their sons or daughters gets reflected and absorbed.

If you can't race and train as seriously as you'd like, there's still room for you. I don't recommend you to ride road races for the simple reason that even the also-rans have to match the pace of the best or fade. There's only a certain amount of joy to be had from trailing in long after the leaders, and the novelty soon palls. Nor is there any point in just sitting in and doing your best to hang on: you're just deluding yourself, neutralizing the race and, probably, keeping out someone who'd like to have ridden but couldn't because the field was restricted.

You *can* ride time trials satisfactorily, though, because you'll be riding only against yourself. I'll give you an example. I rode a '50' on the Bath Road one Easter and I felt really pleased with myself, because I'd got close to my personal best

Professional madison handsling. Team-mates link hands as the rider on the inside flies by; the faster rider then heaves his team-mate into the battle. Remember to hold the centre of your bars as you throw your mate or you'll throw yourself as well. The rules don't always allow handslings in amateur races. The technique there is to grab your team-mates shorts as you pass.

Madisons started as a way round the law – a two-man race thought up at Madison Square Garden. The picture's a good illustration, too, of track markings. From the inside, the first line marks the point around which the track is measured. In many events there's no advantage in going below it, but for championships and record attempts, the line would be re-inforced with small sandbags. Above it, the paler line shows the lowest point on the track at which it's permissible to overtake a rider on the inside. The line round the middle shows the same thing for motor-paced rides, but it's also used in a madison as a boundary for 'resting' riders, waiting to be reached by their team-mates. The classic beginner's error on a track is to get his front wheel inside the back wheel ahead – a sure way of getting trapped and crashing.

despite rain and gales. As I walked to the results board with a glow of personal satisfaction, I realized with horror that the winner, Bob Porter, had beaten me by twenty minutes. In other words, he could have ridden an extra ten miles in the same time. But I still bet he wasn't as satisfied with his ride as I was with mine. With time trials you don't even have to enter open events, because many clubs run their own, or combine to form promoting organizations.

If you can't get road racing out of your system, there's a diluted substitute in long-distance riding in Audax events. These are what these days replace reliability trials – set distances, usually in multiples of 100km, within minimum and maximum times. The maximum time is quite generous, and the minimum time may seem to keep the maximum speed too low. In fact, given the way the clock keeps running during food stops over 200, 300, 400 and even 600km, there's plenty of opportunity to hare along.

One of the keenest Audax riders, John Richardson, told me on my first 300km that 'any decent rider can cover the distance, so the only satisfaction is in seeing how close you can get to the minimum time.' I thanked him very much and said I'd be happy to finish the distance in any time.

The other option is cyclo-cross. I don't know why I haven't ridden more, because they're much more fun than anything else I've ever ridden. My first, the Bagshot Scramble, had me in giggles from whooping up and down sandy hills. I was working for *Cycling* at the time, so the comments of spectators were worth hearing. Do try a cyclo-cross, because even if you're lapped several times, as I was, it doesn't matter because all races are over a set time (an hour and five laps, say) and everyone finishes once the winner has crossed the line. No trailing in ages afterwards.

As for the track, I'm afraid there's so little racing these days that your chances depend entirely on where you live. You'll need special equipment, of course, and it's worth having a go if you live near a midweek league. But remember that track riding calls for a lot of skill and you'll need a fair bit of training before you stop being a danger to the others.

Cyclo-cross – a wonderful all-round winter activity for bike riders. Thoroughly recommended.

There are few world-class tracks in Britain, a sign perhaps of how track racing here has dwindled. This is Leicester, now resurfaced in wood.

3 ON YOUR BIKE

You can spend a fortune on a bike, or you can get by on budget equipment. I think in the end there's a much greater difference in the price than in what it will actually do for you. Better equipment is lighter, it is true, and certainly the established market leaders turn out gear that wears less and lasts longer, but it also costs more.

I argue that you might as well buy what you can afford and then ride as fast as you can. By the time you're pretty good and the minute differences in equipment could mean success or failure, you'll be getting the stuff free anyway.

What is more important at this stage is to make sure that what you've got fits you properly, because cycling is a unique blend of physiology and mechanics and if you don't get the leverage right you're wasting effort and not fulfilling your potential.

Cyclists have known this for a long time, of course, but they've also taken a long time to get around to working out what, on the face of it, should be a perfectly straightforward mathematical relationship between limb length and bicycle size.

That's the problem to which researchers at Loughborough applied themselves in 1965. They knew that it was easy to work out which part of a muscle's range has the greatest output in one-off movements, but it was altogether different to consider groups of muscles working together and alternating between prime movers (those doing the work) and antagonists (those working in the opposite direction).

They brought 100 riders to their laboratories, ranging from a world champion to novices. To be precise, they had three novices, 21 juniors, 20 third category riders, 30 second category, 20 first category, two national champions, one world champion and three women.

Like most bikies today, most had settled their saddle height almost by chance.

A good balanced position is essential for minimal wasted effort and lasting comfort. Legs should be almost straight at full length; your knees and your elbows should be within or near touching range; your top tube should come between your knees when your cranks are horizontal. There's a trend towards higher saddle heights.

They were reluctant to change what they'd become used to. There wasn't even much common ground. The world champion, Tom Simpson, rode lower than normal and reckoned other riders were sitting too high. Norman Sheil thought they were mostly too low.

One by one, the riders rode an ergometer set at different heights and different resistances. Eventually it became clear that the nearer riders were to setting their saddles at 109 per cent of their inside leg length, the better they were doing.

You can find the details in the college library at Loughborough. Among them you'll find that even a small variation from 109 per cent – which was considered a ludicrous height and much ridiculed in the cycling press – caused quite a fall-off in performance. As little as four per cent change brought a marked decline.

Interestingly, there was also a general (although far from absolute) link between a rider's record and his saddle height. The better his category, the nearer he was likely to be what the boffins reckoned was his ideal saddle height.

Even now, though, most riders do no more than sit on a bike, raise the saddle until their legs are just a little bent at full stretch, tighten the seat pin and ride away.

This haphazard method irritated Cyrille Guimard, the manager who brought Bernard Hinault, Greg LeMond and others to their greatest prominence. With a French physiologist, he used the wind tunnel at the Renault car plant to test 15 of the company's team. He discovered that the method produced a saddle that was too low, that was inefficient for muscles, and less aerodynamic.

He raised LeMond's saddle an inch and a half. LeMond, remember, had already become world junior road champion and silver medallist in the pursuit.

'That's like increasing your shoe size three sizes,' LeMond says of the increase. 'I was shocked. Although he told me to raise it slowly, I increased my position by the entire inch and a half for just one day to see how it was. It felt as if I could barely touch the pedals. Yet Guimard was right – now the saddle height seems normal.

'Once I got used to it, I realized how much difference the right position makes. Not only did I ride better, but all the muscles in my body loosened up. I never had lower back pain any more, my arms were never sore. Most of all, I was using the muscular force delivered by my legs much more efficiently. This meant that my entire body was better rested at the end of a long race.'

Guimard's system is to measure his rider's leg length, from crotch to floor, and multiply it by .883. He got that figure from his own tests with professional riders. You take the measurement without shoes, right from the ground and pressing the tape firmly but not violently into the soft tissue which sits on the saddle. In other words, you try to simulate the pressure of weight on the saddle.

That distance, multiplied by .883, is the correct distance between the dip in the saddle to the centre of your bottom bracket spindle. Guimard argues that this, with Campagnolo pedals, medium-thickness cycling shoes and 170mm cranks, is the ideal setting.

Of course, using a figure like .883 is going to produce saddle heights with extraordinary precision. That's because Guimard started off with a precisely calculated average, but the tolerance in saddle height by his system has to be a centimetre either way because of all the other variables – the give in your saddle, variations in foot angle and so on. And anyway, you'll change your position repeatedly as you ride.

Once you start looking for ways to calculate saddle height, you soon realize that they produce inconsistent results. The thing that they all reveal, though, is that most riders would gain by raising their saddles. I suggest you use both the Guimard and the Loughborough methods and see how much of a change they'd require. Both will feel awkward at first, especially if you make the alterations too quickly.

Muscles learn to work in set positions, even wrong positions, and they need to be re-educated. Don't turn a long teaching session into a crammer – change the height by an eighth of an inch a week, and ride as often as you can between changes.

Shoeplates

Fitting shoeplates – or cleats, as the American catalogues have it – was once an exasperating job. There was no real alternative to simply trying to nail them in line with the marks that pedals left on the sole of the shoe. But that way it was too easy for things to go wrong: riding without shoeplates in order to leave a sole mark allows the shoes to slide forward to touch the toeclips, so that the mark tends to be too far back down the shoe. And then there's always the risk of getting the shoeplate skew-whiff as you nail it in place. It was generally easier to put up with a wonky shoeplate than it was to refit it.

Now good racing shoes come with shoeplates fitted. They do have to be adjustable, though, so you need to make sure that they are, and that the adjusting bolt isn't so vulnerable that it will wear and become unusable as soon as you start walking.

The plate should be in the centre of the shoe, directly under the ball of the foot. The groove should slot over the rear plate of the pedal so that the pedal axle is exactly under the ball of your foot. To have your foot further forward gives the illusion of greater power; to have it further back decreases pressure but gives fractionally faster acceleration, a combination that some track sprinters prefer.

Take trouble to get your plate position right, because your comfort and the wellbeing of your knees will depend on it. Carry the allen key with you until you get the position right. Never race in new, untried shoes.

Some riders prefer their heels tipped slightly inwards, but remember that, as with all things to do with bike settings, extremes are always wrong.

Fore and Aft

There is only one position for your saddle. It has to be flat and positioned in such a way that the back of your kneecap is over the pedal axle at its most forward point. Anything else will cost you power and might hurt your knees.

Start by moving the saddle as far back as it'll go, and set the top level – place a spirit level on the top tube (crossbar) to check that *it* is flat, and then again across the top of the saddle, resting on the nose and the cantle, tilting the saddle until the bubble rests in just the same place.

Climb back on your bike and set the cranks horizontal (get somebody to check, because it's difficult to get it right for yourself). Hold both brakes on and push on the pedal. Now get your friend to hold a weighted string or a proper plumb line from the hollow at the back of your knee cap. Measure how far the line drops behind the pedal spindle and move your saddle forward by the same amount. Retighten the saddle and keep repeating until you've got it right.

There's a trend for frames to be steeper and steeper. It seems to go one degree every decade – 71 degrees in the 1950s, 72 in the 1960s, 73 in the 1970s and 74 in the 1980s. It's now reached the stage where you have to push the saddle all the way back even to get close to the right position. Sadly, it's better to be slightly too far back than any amount too forward. You waste a lot of effort if you're too forward, whereas being a shade further back can be a little better for long climbs. If you're too far forward, all you can do is hope the shop's got a saddle that'll slide back more – otherwise you're in the market for a shallower frame.

Incidentally, always set the height of the saddle before you try to set it fore and aft; raising the saddle will move it backwards, particularly on frames with shallow angles.

Forward Reach

The one remaining position – that of your handlebars – is more personal. The tops must be lower than the saddle, of course, but the length of the stem depends on the length of the top tube and the height of the frame.

There are two rough guides. First, a frame of the right height for you will bring the top tube between your knees when your cranks are horizontal. And second, the right handlebar adjustment will bring your elbows about an inch ahead of your knees when you're in a comfortable, streamlined position, holding the inside of the bends.

These are only rough guides. They work for most people, but not perfectly on a frame smaller than 21 inches or more than 23. That's because it's hard to get everything right geometrically with large and, especially, with small frames. Tall riders may have rather more than an inch between knees and elbows; short riders would have their bars only fractionally lower than their saddle.

There are national preferences, too. Look at some of the top riders and you can often guess their nationality from their handlebar positions. The Dutch and Belgians favour shorter positions because they race most on short circuit races (such as criteriums) without hills. They're further over the front wheel in a semi-sprinting position. French and British riders are more stretched.

Gear Size

Riding position changes with gear size. Sitting back lets you use the muscles of your backside more, which means you can push your way up a long hill. But that's only on a lowish gear and at a steady speed, because it's not an aerodynamic position.

To flog a gear on the flat, on the other hand, will bring you further forward – riding on the rivet, as some people call it. You're sacrificing a little muscular efficiency in your legs for greater use of your back and arms. It's a strength exercise and a rather tiring one, which is why some riders use it in 25s but not in 12-hours.

There have always been riders who have used bigger gears, and sometimes to good effect. Actually, it's probably better to talk not of big gears but of slow pedalling, since the size of a gear is relative to the speed at which it's being ridden – in other words, a gear that seems big going *up* a hill will seem very low going down the other side.

Slow revving reached a peak in the 1970s when time trialists bought ever larger chainrings and searched for courses with more traffic to suck them along. You could see riders struggling in gears so enormous that it meant that their leg pressure was

Study in streamlining; the faster you go, the harder it is to push the air aside. A classic time-trial position gets Ian Cammish down low and lets him use his powerful arms; a straight back also means he can keep his head up to see where he's going.

lifting them slightly off the saddle rather than depressing the pedals.

The problem was that they were breaking records – or at least a few of them were – so coaches who threw up their hands in horror were met with derisive laughter. When Norman Sheil broke the competition record for 25 miles around 25 years ago, he did it on a single fixed gear in the region of 86 inches, perhaps a shade more. His time would still be respectable today. But in 20 years, the increases in gear size had gone beyond all common sense in relation to the tiny improvement they were bringing.

I respect Sheil's common-sense attitude to things, so I think it's worth repeating what he wrote at the height of the controversy, because it's still relevant now.

'The other day,' he said, 'somebody asked me why I was so anti-gear in time trials. The point is, I'm not. Neither am I anti-time trial. In fact, I don't think I'm anti-anything. If a rider wants to use a gear of 100 plus, who am I to stop him?

'What does upset me, however, is the fact that riders will blandly follow fashion without thinking what they are doing and why they are doing it, and this to me is

Quick releases are wonderful gadgets, but the levers can catch in spokes and pedals. Always push them shut so that they're shielded (but not obstructed) by the frame.

very wrong. The fact that riders have accepted the idea that big gears are the answer to fast times would indicate that they are still looking for the magic formula to success – the easy way.

'First of all, if a rider wants to use a gear of 100 inches or more, he must realize that this entails primarily a strength exercise, and should be treated as such. Few people would be foolish enough to attempt anything that requires a greater strength than they possess, yet you find that bike riders do it every week.

'Quite honestly, I would like to see a rider properly trained with the sole object of using big gears for time trialling. The result, I know, would put the whole problem in its right perspective and riders would immediately realize that there is more to this game than meets the eye.

'He would produce his sub-50-minute "25", not necessarily on a float morning and a super-fast course, but on any reasonable course and decent morning. Now this to me is sense; blindly following other people's techniques (for this is all they are) is wrong.'

Pedal Revs

Now, there's no doubt that your pedalling rate falls with age. Part of this is forced, because the rules apply limited gears in road and track races for under-19s. At the other end, most riders find their revving ability falling from about 40 onwards. Within that range, there has to be an optimum.

Well, cycling is little more than geared walking. You swing your legs gently if you're strolling; you rev slowly if you're just pootling along on a bike. Similarly, your brisk walking rate – about 90 strides a minute – will be much the same as your brisk pedalling rate. Think in those terms and you get your pedalling rate about right.

The difference with cycling, though, is that you have gears to vary your pedalling rate in relation to your road speed – you can pedal slowly at speed, or you can twiddle at walking pace. Naturally, the boffins have had a go at the problem.

Vaughan Thomas, one of the physiologists involved with the saddle-height experiments, established that bike riders have a cadence (movement) rate of 90–120, rather faster than oarsmen (35–40), swimmers (40–50, arms), canoeists (40–50), walkers (75–85) and runners (55–65). It convinced him that cyclists were pedalling too rapidly. In *Science and Sport*, he says: 'Because pedalling machines were the easiest to set up in laboratories, cycling became the main subject of these (cadence) investigations, and a whole stream of suggestions came forth over the years that cyclists would perform more efficiently when pedalling at rates anywhere between 30 and 60 a minute. However, racing cyclists have never been ones to swallow everything boffins tell them, and they went on their way happily pedalling at between 90 and 120 revolutions a minute.

'My own feeling is that cyclists tend to be under-geared, to use too high a cadence rate than is *physiologically* sound.'

Now, what applies on a scientist's pedalling machine might be different from your needs on a bike. Your car might drive most efficiently in top gear, but it overtakes fastest in third. The same applies in a road race or group training, where a lower gear is better for intermittent pedalling in a bunch and for responding to sudden changes of pace. When a small break goes, riders use higher gears because, like time trialists, they're interested in steady fast cruising.

The chances are that slower pedalling, as the boffins recommend, is indeed better for time trialling. Higher gears can be rolled, and there's more time to use shoeplates and toestraps as well as downward pressure. It was that discovery that triggered off the windmill-gear revolution of the 1970s. Jacques Anquetil rode a higher gear to win the Tour de France time trials, and before long so did everybody else. Sometimes revs fell lower than a 60 a minute, although I doubt whether they ever reached 30 on the flat. Even the great Eddy Merckx, one of the strongest all-rounders, was moved to criticize the trend.

The gear you choose is a combination of your age, the race, your strength and your experience. Think of the walking analogy, but remember that the gears are there to be used creatively and not just to maintain a constant revving speed. And remember, too, that the more you roll a higher gear, the more you will be committing yourself to that one skill; you will become a talented time trialist, but you might just be riding into a sporting cul-de-sac. Many all-rounders and committed road riders have won important time trials, but it only works occasionally the other way round.

Steve Snowling, a British mechanic at the Rotterdam Six, starts the lonely job of getting everything ready for the day ahead. In a track race, the bikes are at least clean; after a tour stage, they can be filthy and in need of repair.

4 FULL SPEED AHEAD

So far we have been concentrating on endurance – the stamina you need to complete the race at a good speed. But it's absolute speed that wins races. It doesn't have to be the 20-minute hammering that Bob Porter gave me on the Bath Road that Easter; it could be an imperceptible increase that meant you lost the division road race championship and someone else won it.

That difference could be tiny – a break can go on a corner, on a hill. Or a rider can come by you in the last 200 yards. Speed has beaten you, but the difference in speed between you was kept up for only a flash.

Speed is a combination of things. You need strength – or more strictly, power – to accelerate hard, to jump. You need skill. And you need a very high level of endurance to push back the inevitable onset of oxygen debt. So let's look more closely at that.

Your muscles will work all-out for around 12 seconds before total oxygen debt comes on. You might not have to stop, but you will need to ease up. But you won't go into oxygen debt until your blood system can no longer cope with the demands.

Endurance training has improved your oxygen uptake, toned up the blood distribution, opened unused blood vessels in your muscles, and taught your brain and muscles the skill of efficient pedalling. From there on, you depend on the power of your heart to get blood out quickly.

Your heart has a muscle that contracts violently and squeezes blood from the chambers. You've made those chambers larger; now you need to make the muscle stronger. Once again the overload effect comes in.

Blood has weight, and working the heart hard is weight-training. The muscle thickens and strengthens just like your leg muscles.

Maximum Heart Rates

I've spoken loosely of that effect starting at about 120 beats a minute and increasing as heart rate increases. Now it's time to be more precise. The fastest a young, healthy heart will beat is about 215 strokes a minute. It may not be efficient at that speed – the chambers may not open and close fully – but that's the maximum. The rate falls as you get older, and you can find your own approximate maximum very simply by subtracting your age from 215. The improvement starts at 65 per cent of that figure.

If you're 25, your maximum will be 190 and strengthening will start at 123. If you're 45, your maximum will be 170 and your training threshold 110. The nearer you get to the maximum, the more your training will strengthen your heart rather than enlarge it. That's why speed training has so much short-distance, high-intensity sprinting, such short rests and such a concentration on heart rates.

The clearest evidence is in what the different types of training do for you, shown in the table below.

Method of training	Speed	Cruising	Endurance and stress	Recovery	Skill
Steady state	●	●	●●●●●	●	●●
Group	●●●	●●●	●●●	●●	●●●●
Kermesse	●●●●	●●●	●	●●	●●●●
Interval sprints	●●●●●●	●●●●●	●●●	●●●●	●●
Gym training: Circuits	●	●●●●●	●●●●●●	●●	
Weights	●●●	●●	●●●●●	●●●	

Interval Sprints

The furthest you can maintain top speed is around 200 metres. It will take 12–15 seconds from a rolling start and that's the furthest you can go anaerobically. That's all-out effort, and it'll get your heart close to its maximum.

The distance may be short but it doesn't matter, because the training effect will continue even after you've stopped. Provided you're at 65 per cent or more of your maximum heart rate, it doesn't matter whether you're riding or lying down – your heart is still doing its weight training. Make sure you're thoroughly warmed up, and then sprint 200 yards. Don't worry about style or shattering yourself – just sprint like crazy for 200 yards, neither more nor less. Don't ease up in the slightest until you've crossed the line. Then brake hard and take your recovery time by sticking the tips of a finger and your thumb just under the angle of your jawbone, beneath your ears. That's where you'll find the carotid artery.

Count the beats over six seconds and see how long they take to get back to a tenth of your training threshold. For a 25-year-old, the threshold will be 123 beats a minute, so you're looking for a fall to 12 beats in six seconds (don't worry about fractions because your counting won't be that accurate). It's easier to get a friend or

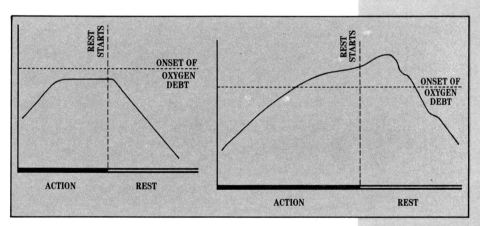

When you're getting as much oxygen as you need, your heart rate rises, steadies, and then slows steadily once you stop.
As soon as you get into oxygen debt, though, your heart rate continues to rise even after you've stopped. And then the rate of recovery is much more ragged.

a coach to do this, by the way. You may notice something odd. You may find, as you count the beats every six seconds, that you count more and more at first instead of fewer and fewer. That's because your heart rate may very well go *up* after oxygen debt. Your recovery gets ragged because your heart and lungs are fighting to repay the debt and neutralize the blood acids and also to keep the rest of the body alive. This is one good reason to make sure your endurance training is done well. You now have a standard recovery time for your interval sprinting. You'll need to re-establish it before every session because it'll vary as you get fitter and also according to your mood, the weather and your tiredness. The overall trend, though, should be a gradual reduction.

Wait until your breathing has recovered and repeat the 200-yard sprint. Relax for exactly your standard recovery time and sprint again. Repeat this for four sprints. After four sprints, relax until your breathing (not just your heart) has recovered. Carry on until you've ridden four sets of four sprints. Then go off and do some steady state training. You won't feel like it, but you'll be quite capable of it once you've calmed down a bit.

You'll have gathered several things by now: that interval sprinting is exceptionally hard work (which is why so many riders ignore it); that it's monotonous (but it also doesn't take very long); and that it's a pain in the neck taking recovery times (much better to take a mate who can use his long recovery periods between sets of sprints to time you during *your* sprints).

Before long, you'll be able to step up the training level by riding five sets of four sprints, then six sets, and so on. But remember that the whole purpose is defeated if you don't give the sprinting everything you've got or if you don't stop completely during the brief rest periods.

Kermesse Sprints

Do try pure interval sprinting, because it'll show you how much or how little rest you need between sprints. But once you know that figure, you could alleviate the monotony of sprinting backwards and forwards by kermesse sprinting.

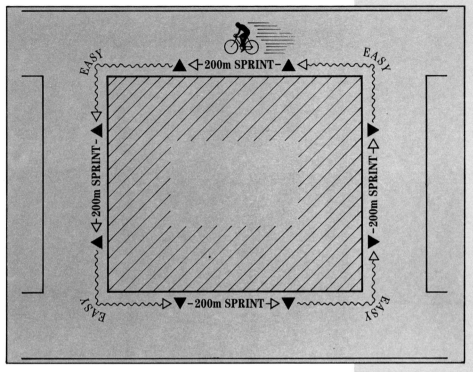

Kermesse sprinting: very effective but very monotonous, too.

Traditionally, kermesses were held round village squares while the annual funfair (the *kermesse*, in French) was in progress in the middle. Square is the operative word, because the exercise consists of sprinting out of corners.

What you need is a safe square, each side about 500 yards. Warm up round the circuit, sprint for 200 yards out of one corner, brake hard and freewheel at walking pace to the next corner. Sprint out of that and carry on until you've finished the square. Rest as before and repeat.

The rest intervals between sprints are much less accurate, so the precise benefits aren't measurable, but the effect is still considerable. By the way, train on the circuit with someone else, by all means, but never match-sprint together, because if you do the better rider probably won't train hard enough and the weaker one will start giving up.

Ladder Sprints

Another variation, even less precise but also useful, is the ladder sprint. It's particularly effective up a gentle climb, and it brackets all sorts of intervals and sprinting distances. This makes it a clumsy tool, but it's very demanding.

Choose a long straight road, level or slightly uphill, and mark off a starting point. A road with lamp-posts is ideal because you can sprint for two lamp-posts and ride very gently back to the start; then sprint three lamp-posts, then four, then five, then six, each time riding back gently to the start.

There's no point in sprinting for less than ten seconds or for more than fifty, so arrange your ladder accordingly. Once you've sprinted all the way up the ladder, start again, this time with decreasing distances.

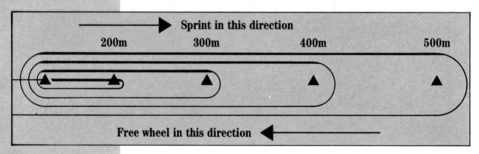

Ladder sprinting – a combination of sprint distance and recuperation periods.

A Word of Warning

Years ago, when I first took my coaching exams, I was persuaded that interval training was the one and only true gospel. It shone from the clouds like a message I was to tell the world. A few months later I met Dr Peter Travers, at St Luke's College in Exeter, where he ran a physiology lab. And what he told me changed my mind, particularly so far as riders under about 17 are concerned.

Dr Travers pointed out, as he already had to education authorities, that young people's hearts are still growing in the way that the rest of them is growing. If you thicken a heart muscle a great deal, it won't stretch to take in more blood when you start endurance training. What's more, Travers argued, children running about at

Too much interval training and too little steady-state will give you a tight heart with a very powerful muscle (top line). Too much steady-state and too few intervals will give you a large heart which can't contract powerfully (vertical line).
A good combination (diagonal line) gives you volume *and* power.

school are effectively interval training well enough already without having enthusiastic but misguided coaches introducing even more on such a tough and systematic basis.

I don't think any rider should concentrate obsessively on interval training – speed is important, naturally, but endurance figures higher in most races – and I'm more and more persuaded that under-17s shouldn't do much, if any, formal interval sprinting at all. Much better, at that age, to make sure that group training contains plenty of intensive work and variety. Endurance intervals, certainly.

For everybody else, though – sorry, no excuses!

A Twitch in Time

You've maybe wondered why some cyclists are good sprinters and others are naturally good distance riders. Build helps, of course – sprinting is a strength sport which favours stocky riders with heavy muscles. But that doesn't explain why sprinters are appalling time trialists.

Well, here's the answer.

In simple terms, your muscles are made up of two types of fibre. They're arranged in bundles which contract and creep over each other when an electrical charge trickles down a nerve. The creeping makes the muscle shorten and move a limb.

Your thigh muscles, for example, are fixed to your shin just below your knee-cap – you can feel the tendon and the enlarged head of the shinbone where they join. Tighten your thighs and the muscle pulls your leg straight. The hamstring muscles at the back work the same way but in the opposite direction, shortening and bending your knee.

Not all the muscle fibres contract at once. Joints like the knee couldn't stand the strain if they did. Your leg would snap. What governs how many fibres contract are the strength of the electrical charge and the susceptibility of the fibres. The more the bundles that shorten, the stronger the movement.

You can't change the number of bundles, but many physiologists say that by training you can make them more susceptible to electrical charges. But you would tire very quickly if that was all that was going on, so there has to be a second control.

The two different fibres are red and white. Red ones have a lot of myoglobin, which stores oxygen. That means they'll work away steadily for a long time so long as they're being fed with oxygen – the perfect aerobic fibre. They take a tenth of a second to tighten, so they're commonly known as slow-twitchers.

White fibres – they're pale rather than white – twitch in only a fifth of the time, which makes them tire quickly. But to make up for that, they're good in oxygen debt.

Training makes both slow- and fast-twitch fibres work better, but you can't change the proportion of each. The longer the race (especially in time trials, because the tactics and hills of road racing distort the picture), the more slow-twitchers you need – around 80 per cent, perhaps. Sprinters need many more fast-twitchers. All-rounders have an even balance. So, it's no coincidence that sprinters and stayers, road riders and time trialists are so different in style and character.

You could have a lump cut out and checked at a hospital, of course, but science usually confirms what we already know. If you've been riding more than a year or two and you're moderately fit, I think you'll have long ago realized whether you're by nature a sprinter or a 24-hour rider.

5 GETTING IT ORGANIZED

There's no one schedule guaranteed to bring succeess. There are only so many variables, but you are about as likely to need the same training schedule as someone else as you are to look exactly like him. That's why I get so cross about the 'Train my way . . .' articles that used to appear – not only were a lot of them pretty ill-informed, but there was no reason why they would necessarily suit anyone else anyway.

The advent of the coaching scheme and the realization that physiology applies to cycling as much as any other sport have done a lot to change things. I can teach you training techniques, and I can tell you what effect they will have, but only you can decide how to balance them to your own best advantage. First consider everything that's involved:

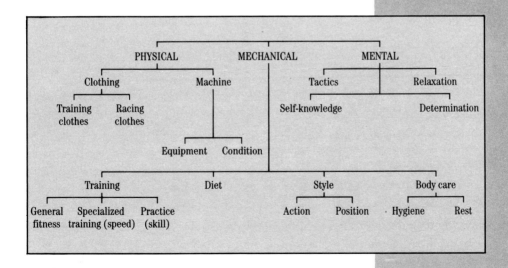

Then there are your targets – what you can feasibly achieve. You can't win the Tour de France on one or even two six-week training schedules. And, although nobody has reached the limit of human performance – if they had, records would stop falling – some people have further to go than others. Training will make you better, but never get downhearted if it turns out there isn't a Sean Kelly or Francesco Moser inside you. On the other hand, by all means have a burning ambition, and set a worthwhile target.

Another factor is the amount of time you've got. Professionals can train longer, and they can rest longer as well. They don't have other jobs, whereas you may have a career or at least a weekly wage to worry about. You will suffer physically and mentally if you cram in too much.

Training Circle

You need to set two training circles – one for the whole year, one for the racing season – and a chart for six weeks' training.

Until recently, even good riders stopped racing and training at the end of the season and had a good boozy time until the new year. Then, with great distress, they started training. I remember an old French professional telling me it was essential because the muscles needed a break and the mind did as well. The second point I accept, but the first I never can.

Your body is a machine, just like a racing car. Tune a racing car daily and it will perform beautifully; neglect it for a week, let alone months, and it will deteriorate. Any machine will run down if it's not used continually, let alone one like your body which can adjust itself to conditions.

On the other hand, you have a brain which craves variety. And the weather changes. You'd go barmy if you trained the same way all year, and you'd skid about on the ice, anyway. My advice is to keep riding all winter – get out in a group and get to love cycling as a wonderful social sport; ride cyclo-cross, a tremendous way to keep up the pressure, and have a good laugh with nothing at stake (unless you want to specialize, in which case you turn everything on its ear).

Spend part of the winter in the gym, trying circuit and weight training. The first improves your oxygen uptake and mental endurance, the second obviously improves your strength. But bearing in mind that you get exactly what you train for, you have to be riding your bike pretty frequently or there'll be no crossover and all you'll become is a good circuit trainer or a good weight trainer (and please note that I'm talking about weight training, which is smaller weights lifted many times for power, and not weight lifting, which is heavy weights lifted only once or twice for strength).

When someone asked Norman Sheil whether it was worth going to circuit-training classes, he said: 'If you mean "Does it make me go faster?" then the answer is no. If you mean "Does it make me fitter?" then the answer is yes.

'Circuit training does not make you a better bike rider. It is an exercise to develop the heart and lungs, and because of this you are more able to handle hard cycle racing when the time comes. Unfortunately, too many riders feel that the work they have done in the winter has no bearing on their fitness during the summer. Yet when you question them, you find that they have achieved a higher degree of fitness which not only comes quicker but is longer lasting.'

Circuit training is a round of exercises which keep a constant pressure on the heart and lungs but spread the effort round the body. So a leg exercise might be followed by an arm exercise, then a stomach exercise, and so on. You can get details of classes for cyclists from the British Cycling Federation. Lists are also published once or twice a year in *Cycling Weekly*.

If you can't find a class, try another sport. Avoid football and rugby, because the attitude and aura are quite different. But the other sports are great. If nothing else, they'll stop you becoming a cycling bore. Gerard Daniëls, a Belgian doctor specializing in cycling, identifies the benefits of the different sports as follows:

Athletics	*sprinting* – muscle power and co-ordination
	mid-distance – recovery
	distance – stamina

	jumping – muscle power and co-ordination *throwing* – muscle power
Badminton	co-ordination
Basketball	co-ordination and muscle power
Boxing	co-ordination and a little muscle power
Handball	muscle power and co-ordination
Hockey	stamina
Judo	muscle power and co-ordination
Canoeing	endurance
Rowing	*short-distance* – muscle power *long-distance* – stamina and recovery
Rugby	muscle power and stamina
Table tennis	co-ordination
Tennis	muscle power and co-ordination
Gymnastics	strength and co-ordination
Football	*outdoor* – strength and stamina *indoor* – co-ordination
Volleyball	muscle power and co-ordination
Water polo	muscle power and stamina
Wrestling	muscle power
Swimming	*short-distance* – muscle power *mid-distance* – recovery *long-distance* – stamina and recovery *diving* – co-ordination

Don't under-rate co-ordination, by the way. It's not usually something of which cyclists can be proud!

Weight training is a great way of gaining not only *extra* strength but *general* strength. Too many bike riders have strong legs but weak backs and arms, so that some of the benefits are lost. You need an expert to teach you weight training, because it's dangerous done the wrong way. Use a qualified coach, or go to organized training classes. Here, though, are the basics: These are the basic movements – but you'll need a coach to tell you how many sets of movements and which weights would be best for you.

Bar lift

Slip a 20lb disc on each end and, as with all these exercises, make sure it's fixed securely, that you have firm footing and strong shoes, and that there are no obstructions. Jump around for several minutes to warm up.

1. Walk up to the bar, place your shoelaces under it and your feet at shoulder width. Keep your head up and your shoulders back (stare straight ahead; don't look down).

2. Bend your knees and reach down with straight arms. Your arms should go outside your knees. Grasp the bar with your knuckles forward, straighten your knees and stand up.

Lowering it is exactly the reverse procedure; try it several times at the start of all weight training.

Behind neck press

1. Lift to thigh height, pause. 2. Continue to chest height, pause, and flick your wrists back to support the weight (knuckles back towards you). 3. Push the bar up carefully and lower it to sit across the top of your shoulders. 4. Push your arms straight upwards, breathing in; pause, breathe out and lower to your shoulders.

Power clean
1. Lift the bar to thigh height, overhand. 2. Pause and continue to chin height, as in the first stage of the behind neck press. Flip the weight back in your hands, hold a second, then return to the ground. This should be a smooth, almost continuous movement.

Bent-over rowing
Never do this without expert guidance, because it's dangerous done wrongly.
1. Approach the bar and grasp overhand. Make the small of your back as hollow as possible; stick your bottom out and flex your spine into a banana shape. 2. Lift the bar to chest height, breathing in; lower to arm's length, breathing out. Never use your back muscles to lift the weight.

Brench press
You'll need a firm, old fashioned bench for this. Lie along the bench with your head supported and your knees bent and feet firmly on the floor.
1. Get two helpers to hand you a loaded bar; grasp it overhand and hold it just clear of your chest (never over your throat or face). 2. Push the bar upwards, pause, and lower.
Your helpers must stay nearby in case you get into difficulty, and also to take the weight away when you've finished.

1

2

Squat jump
Not quite as good as leg presses, but an alternative. Not for anyone under 23 because it will compress an immature spine.
1. Place the bar across your shoulders as in the behind neck press. Bend your knees carefully to halfway between a standing and sitting position.
2. Then jump as high as you can.

1

2

Leg press
A great exercise for bike riders, but you can do it only with special equipment. The principle is simple – just get well under the weights platform, grasp the supports, and push upwards.
Do make sure the weights are firmly attached and that there are safety stops to prevent the platform sliding down and crushing you.

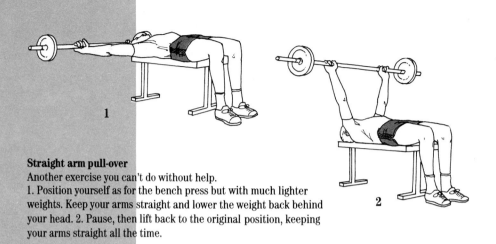

Straight arm pull-over
Another exercise you can't do without help.
1. Position yourself as for the bench press but with much lighter
weights. Keep your arms straight and lower the weight back behind
your head. 2. Pause, then lift back to the original position, keeping
your arms straight all the time.

Standing curl
1. Lift the bar as in the initial lift, but with an
underhand grasp – with your fingers forward.
2. Pause, keep your back upright and firm, then
bend your arms to raise the bar to chin height.
3. Pause and lower.

Sit-up
Sit on the floor with your ankles almost together
and your knees a little bent. Hook your feet under
something firm, place your hands behind your
neck and lift your upper body.

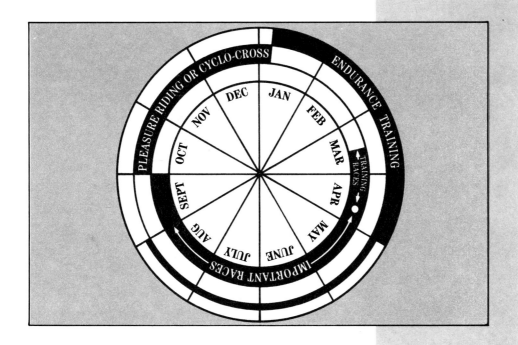

Training Circle 1

Draw yourself a circle and divide it into 12 sectors to represent the months.

Now mark in when you want to start racing and when you first want to make an impact, which should be at least four weeks later. Now start working backwards. You'll need to be well into your endurance training by the time you start racing, and you'll want to add speed training between the first race (or slightly before) and the first target race.

The extent of the endurance training will depend on how long your races are and how fit you are at the moment. Remember that it takes about three weeks to regain every week you've spent off the bike (although the ratio falls as the lay-off increases).

Carry on round the circle, shading in your full racing season, the cyclo-cross season (or as much of it as you want to ride), the weeks in which circuit- and weight-training classes run, and so on. By the time you're finished, you'll have something that looks a bit like this:

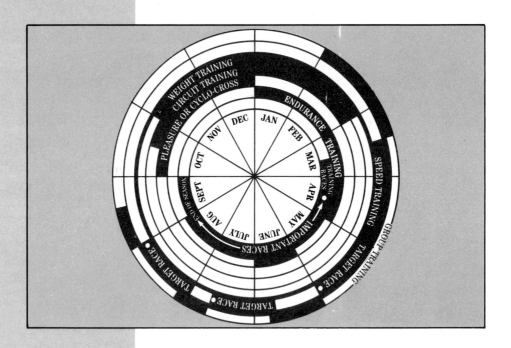

Training Circle 2

Notice that pure speed training isn't necessarily continuous. It's too monotonous and intensive for that, and it doesn't let you build up to peaks of performance. It's replaced between peaks by more group training, but remember that that has to be pretty intensive or you will start getting slower. Swedish coaches have a wonderful word for this kind of training – they call it *fartlek*. Once heard, it's a word never to be forgotten. It means mixing up everything into the same carefree but intensive training session. So you might be sprinting for signs, racing up hills, settling into bit-and-bit sessions – anything, provided it's varied and hard work. I don't speak a word of Swedish, but I'm told that *fartlek* means speedplay, which just about sums it up.

But a word of advice: don't let more than a couple of weeks pass before you start sprint sessions again. Sprinting 'educates' the fast-twitch fibres in your muscles and they need frequent exposure to maintain the knowledge. Otherwise, like everything else, they'll deteriorate.

Six-Week Schedule

Now you can train for an immediate objective. Always set a target that's achievable but which will stretch you, even if you're still in basic training. Think of what's available:

(a) The spare time you've got

(b) The time you'll need for sleep and rest (which increases as you train)

(c) How far from home you'll need to ride to find suitable roads (maybe some distance if you live in a city centre)

(d) A friend or coach to help

(e) Space at home for stretching exercises, or weight training

(f) The equipment you have – have you got a training bike or will you have to allow extra time for modifying your race bike?

(g) The hours you work, and whether you can ride and perhaps train on the way there or back

(h) Whether you can find a coach in the lists published by the BCF and RTTC and whether the coach is the right one and you are the right rider for him

(i) Whether there's a track near enough to be worth considering

Now draw up a table for the next two months . . .

Week	Monday	Tuesday	Wednesday	Thursday	Friday	Saturday	Sunday
1							
2							
3							

. . . and so it goes on.

Now mark in all the days you know you won't be available. Perhaps you work late, or you have an evening class. Mark in any fixed dates, such as weight- and circuit-training classes, crucial races, the nights you meet clubmates to plan your race entries, the night on which the local chaingang rides.

What you're left with is the time you've got for scheduled training. Think about the time of the year, the balance that you need between endurance and speed training; look again at the table on page 7, and this list below by Gerard Daniëls of the attributes needed for the different types of riding:

TRACK RIDERS	
Sprint	exceptional thigh strength
	exceptional co-ordination
	little stamina
	little recovery
Pursuit	exceptional stamina
	very good recovery
	normal muscle power
	normal co-ordination
ROAD RIDERS	
Distance	exceptional stamina
(e.g. classics)	very good recovery
	powerful thigh muscles
	normal co-ordination
Hill climbers	very good stamina
	very good recovery
	very good co-ordination
	normal muscle strength

(There's a considerable difference, by the way, between what we think of as a hill climber and what a Belgian thinks of. Dr Daniëls is thinking of hills like the

Pyrenees and not the very British habit of holding uphill races against the clock in the autumn.)

Now build in the progression that you need, the overload that will increase your fitness. Read through the chapters on endurance and speed training, and the way the sessions have to be built up. Now relate the whole lot to your first big target of the season.

Don't choose too many targets. In time trialling you can look for steady progress through the year, aiming to reach peak fitness for a particular championship, or to switch distances to bring up a good BAR average. In road racing, there are three kinds of event: the ones you ride for training, where you won't let tactics get in the way of good training; those you wouldn't mind winning; and the few races that you

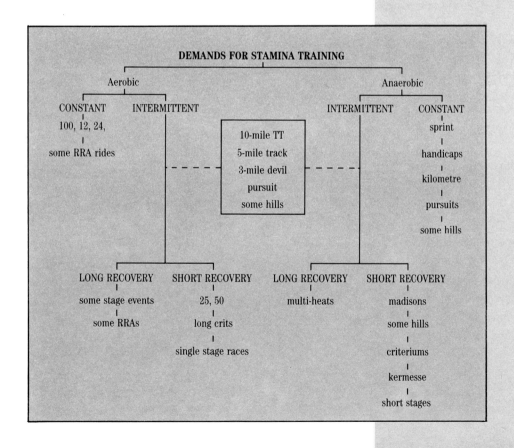

DEMANDS FOR STAMINA TRAINING

Aerobic			Anaerobic	
CONSTANT	INTERMITTENT		INTERMITTENT	CONSTANT
100, 12, 24,				sprint
		10-mile TT		
some RRA rides		5-mile track		handicaps
		3-mile devil		kilometre
		pursuit		
		some hills		pursuits
				some hills

LONG RECOVERY	SHORT RECOVERY	LONG RECOVERY	SHORT RECOVERY
some stage events	25, 50	multi-heats	madisons
some RRAs	long crits		some hills
	single stage races		criteriums
			kermesse
			short stages

really have to win, like a division or national championship. Only you know those targets.

Obviously, if you're racing just for training, there's no reason you shouldn't train the day before as well. If the race is important, a rest or, better still, a short leg-stretcher that won't leave you tired, is better. Before a distant, important race, it is also better, if you can afford it, to stay nearby overnight rather than spend hours cramped in a car after making an early start.

The younger you are, the more I suggest you don't train the day after your race. You're still growing and you need more than the normal rest. Otherwise, try to train as frequently as you can, remembering that there's no worthwhile effect unless you train at least three times a week. If you concentrate on *quality* rather than *quantity*, your training will leave you tired but not exhausted. Tiredness passes, but fatigue lingers.

Overtraining

It usually takes a little experience or the eye of a good coach to spot overtraining. *Under*training is easy to see – you just get beaten in races where you shouldn't be beaten. Overtraining, on the other hand, shows in a combination of tiredness, mental fatigue, possible anaemia and the rest. Some people just call it staleness, but call it what you will, you know it when you've got it. Your drive goes, your morale takes a tumble, and you feel nervous and get bored.

One of the world's top running coaches said he looked for:
- less general resistance, with headaches, sniffles, fever blisters, etc.
- mild leg soreness which occurred from day to day (this is in runners, remember)
- an 'I don't care' attitude towards training and even quite everyday activities
- wanting to pack in races
- a kind of 'hangover' feeling from the previous race and a significant drop in body weight from the day before

You can worry yourself unnecessarily about these things, and that makes matters worse. For that reason I've always recommended riders to keep training diaries.

Write in how you felt, what time you went to bed, how you slept and how long, any minor ailments, your mood, and everything else you did, as well as your training. These diaries soon become great stores of useful information. You can spot trends and causes, see how much sleep suits you, what improvement follows what training. It all helps you know yourself better.

You will soon see how long it takes you to recover from a major effort. You will see that first you get over the original oxygen debt, then the immediate tiredness. But lingering for some days will be the overall fatigue. It could take hours or days to clear, and in all that time your pulse and therefore your general metabolic rate will be faster than usual.

You can check this for yourself. Take your pulse every morning before you sit up, as soon after waking as you can. Count the beats for 15 seconds. Then count again right after you get up. Do it every day, when you don't think you've been overtraining, and compare the difference between the two rates. If there's not much difference, you've got little to worry about, but if there's a marked change, something is wrong.

But don't fret unnecessarily. Remember it's only a guide, that it's too easy to get it wrong. Certainly don't over-react. Audrey McElmury, the former world road race champion, reckons: 'We've heard many people say that they wouldn't train on a particular day because their pulse rate was high. They think this is a result of not being fully recovered from the previous day's training. This may be true, but unfortunately this variation can be due to a multitude of other external things. These may include staying up late, anxiety, sleeplessness, etc.

'What happens on race day if your pulse is up (or any other day)? We feel that you should continue to train unless there are other bodily symptoms indicating being run down or sick. Pulse, if used as a sole indicator of when you can train, can be very misleading, and should be only one of the factors to consider about your physical state.'

What's more, you should toughen your mental outlook so that almost nothing stops you doing the training that you should be doing. You've got an excuse if you're unwell or you can't control changed circumstances, but otherwise you grow a little softer every time you make your training easier than it should be. Erratic training leads to erratic performance.

Anaemia

Scattered around your body is about enough iron to make three paper clips. It doesn't sound much, but you've only got to lose a little and you're in trouble.

The iron is in three main kinds of compound, of which the most important is the chemical that makes blood look red – haemoglobin. This is where the numbers get boggling. Haemoglobin travels in the blood, which is mainly water, in tiny bi-concave discs shaped like Trebor mints. You wouldn't believe how minute they are. There are ten pints of blood in your body, and they carry five million red cells in each cubic millimetre. Each individual cell contains 280 million molecules of haemoglobin. Of those, each haemoglobin molecule contains 10,000 atoms of hydrogen, carbon, oxygen and sulphur – *and just four atoms of iron.*

How can such a minute thing be so important?

Well, it's the iron in your blood that gives it its octane rating. Running an athletic body on blood with too little iron is like trying to race at Brands Hatch on two-star petrol. Too little iron in the blood is called anaemia, and it's bad news for athletes. Cyclists are quite prone to it. When they tested British riders at an Olympic Games, they found most of them were low on iron.

Each red cell is supposed to live for six weeks. It then falls apart and sheds its iron. Some gets kept, and the rest is lost.

For some reason the average life of a red cell in athletes is much shorter. It may have something to do with the battering that the blood gets. Whatever the reason, the loss sometimes comes suddenly. You feel lethargic, your results fall off, you get less enthusiastic, you may get headaches or pins and needles, you may not be able to sleep as well as normally.

Many of these symptoms, of course, will sound familiar if you were paying attention during the section on overtraining. One might well produce the other.

A doctor can arrange a blood test, but the delay will probably be too long. Anyway, it's fairly easily put right provided there's no underlying medical cause. Make sure your diet is right – there's a chapter to come on that. And note these words by Peter Travers: 'Hard training does bring about iron deficiency and is rapidly corrected by taking organic iron – something like Ferrograd C – but . . . it is as well to establish by doing a blood test, and then to control the amount of iron by giving several tests, rather than giving iron wholesale.'

Ferrograd C is effective. It might make you a bit constipated, but it works quickly. But don't rely on any supplement to your diet. Taking iron tablets, for example, could make your digestion lazy – you may get used to the easy doses of iron and lose the habit of extracting it from your food.

If you think you're anaemic and iron tablets don't do the trick within a few days, see your doctor immediately. Persistent anaemia can be a serious condition.

6 YOU ARE WHAT YOU EAT

That title, You Are What You Eat, used to be an advertising slogan of some sort, and quite a slick one. Like all slogans, it's substantially true, but not entirely so. Three general points are worth noting at the outset:

First, apart from smoking, taking drugs and getting pie-eyed on alcohol, there's precious little that is actually bad for you.

Second, carbohydrates aren't bad. They're essential, and much of what you read in slimming diets is tosh so far as bike riders are concerned.

Third, you should never get too fussy about what you eat or you'll never survive away from home.

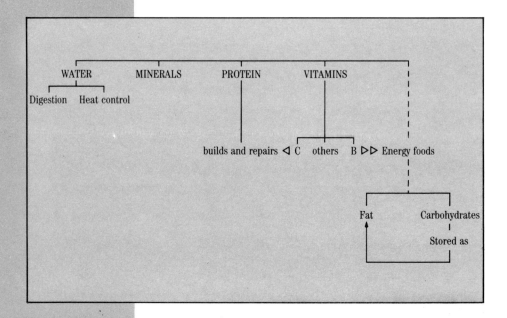

Energy

Your body works on oxygen and sugar, the first from the air, the second from the food that you eat. Simple sugars – like granulated sugar itself, and honey – go straight into the body; complex sugars, like starch from potatoes, have to be broken down, a process that starts in your mouth.

Putting it very simply, you can measure what you eat and the exercise that you take in calories. Take in more than you use and you store enough sugar for two hours' exercise and turn the balance into fat, which is a mobile energy store. Sugar tops up your blood when the glycogen that it stores is running low – that's when you start feeling listless and start working away on your fat reserves. But taking in sugar before you need it has a boomerang effect. You can't handle too much sugar, so your body secretes insulin. That drops the blood sugar almost as quickly as it rose, so you take more sugar and your body gets confused. When you start training you use the sugar store first and then start eating away the fat. The fat's not very efficient at turning into energy, but in the end you whittle it down – provided you don't keep topping up the sugar too much. Sugar's useful to take with you in races, either in lumps or, better, in a glucose drink (glucose is a simple sugar). But beware of becoming a sugar addict.

Don't over-sweeten your race drinks. It's probably better to eat something that's not obviously sugary – like rice or a sandwich – and let it sugar your blood as it

As you work, you use your blood sugar. After two hours, you will have used up your resources and your body will be draining itself. You may also be dehydrated. Your internal temperature is at fever pitch. You are exhausted.
Regular drinking and sensible eating will defer the sensation, known to bikies as 'knock'. But fatigue will get you in the end and only your fitness will determine when and how quickly you'll recover.

breaks down in your digestion, and to drink something just slightly sweetened, like diluted fruit squash. Drinking frequently is important, as you'll see later.

Something else I don't recommend is carbohydrate-loading. You've probably heard of it in athletics. The theory is that you will store more than the usual glycogen if you starve the body of sugars for a few days. You eat the usual amount, but you cut right down on sugars and starches, like bread, potatoes, rice and so on. You also go for a very long training ride to use all the sugar inside you. Then you turn your diet on its head, eating as much as usual but concentrating on sweet things. If you time it right, the theory goes, over-compensation stacks extra sugar in your muscles ready for racing.

I don't recommend it for several reasons. First, it's unpredictable. Second, it places a great deal of stress on you. Third, it holds water in the muscles, making them ache. Fourth, a long race in athletics – a marathon in two hours – is quite short by cycling standards and there's no guarantee of what would happen during four hours of racing. Younger riders already have enough problems coping with growing. (It is different in running, with marathons appealing to adults rather than the under-20s.)

Even so, for the sake of fairness I should tell you that many different sports have used it with success. If you want to try, don't experiment just before an important event, and take expert advice.

Martin Hyman, a top-class runner and sports researcher, said: 'There is overwhelming evidence that competitors in endurance events lasting over two hours of continuous high level of effort will enhance their staying power by using the diet.' Bernard Hinault used carbo-loading to win the Grand Prix des Nations in 1984.

Dr Clyde Williams wrote in March 1973: 'Increasing the glycogen stores in muscle is becoming common practice among endurance athletes. There is good physiological evidence to recommend the use of glycogen-loading techniques as part of the normal preparation for long distance races . . .

'There are certain changes which occur . . . about which the athlete new to this technique might be concerned. The most obvious is the marked increase in body weight . . . Increases of 6–9lb above the weight at the end of the low-carbohydrate period are commonly reported. However, only about a third of the increased body weight can be attributed to glycogen storage because each gramme of glycogen stored is accompanied by 3–4 grammes of water . . . There is a camel-like advantage to carrying the additional water. The water is available, after glycogen depletion, to contribute to prevent dehydration.'

Final word to me, since it's my book: remember that runners, on whom most of the experiments have been carried out, run only a few marathons a year; you, the bike rider, might be riding four-hour races every weekend, perhaps several times a week. There is a difference, especially when it comes to carbo-loading.

Power and Recuperation

The whoomph in your riding comes from sugar, but it's provided by muscles, and the muscles, like everything else, get damaged in the process. The whole system of getting stronger comes from muscle fibres being broken down and then re-building stronger than they were before.

The fibres are built from proteins, which are bewildering compounds containing *amino acids*. Most acids change themselves into whatever you need at the time, but eight won't. They're crucial to your health, so they're called *essential* amino acids. They come in meat, eggs and cheese, which provide what are called first-class proteins.

This gives you a problem if you're a vegetarian, more especially if you're a vegan. You do get both carbohydrates and protein from a vegetarian diet, but most vegetables lack at least one essential amino acid and you might find a protein supplement useful. On the other hand, too many vegetarians have become world-class athletes to suggest that a meatless diet is a severe drawback.

One warning note, though: you might need patience and perseverance on a stage race. The more you race, the less time you have, and the more you eat; finding a vegetarian meal might be hard. This isn't intended to change your beliefs, only to warn you. As Greg LeMond observed: 'I remember racing at Chaiapas, Mexico, as an amateur with the United States national team in 1980. Of six riders on that team, four were vegetarian or very strict with their diet. Two days after arriving there, the four who had special diets became ill, possibly because they had trouble adjusting to a much different diet. Three of them were so bad off that they were put on a plane back to the United States.

'As a professional in Europe, it would be very difficult to be a vegetarian. Because European restaurants serve a lot of meat and often only a few poor-quality vegetables, I have to eat what's available ... A handful of European pros are vegetarians and I have seen them have a hard time getting decent meals when a local restaurant owner proudly displays a meal of sausage as an opener, beef stew, pork chops, and french fries as the main courses. Often the only vegetable around is a sad heap of oversteamed carrots.'

You need protein in proportion to the exercise that you take. But the same applies to everything else. There was a time in the 1950s when team officials connected protein with exercise and concluded that more protein would build more muscle. Hence the stories of peasant families eating shoddy meals as their scrimped money went on steak for their bike-rider son. But it didn't work, except psychologically, because you can't store protein. You can turn a little into energy, but it's difficult and wasteful, and the rest disappears.

Vitamins

Casimir Funk, a Polish chemist, discovered vitamins shortly before the Second World War. He was stuck for a name, scratched his head, and decided that they were essential for life (*vita*) and that he'd discovered an amine. Hence vitamin.

Boffins discovered more vitamins and gave them names, but the names were complicated, so they gave them code letters as well: vitamin A, vitamin B, and so on. When they found sub-classes, they gave them numbers, such as B_1 and B_{12}.

Scientists are still working out what exactly vitamins do. It's easier to say what will happen without them. They're catalysts, which make other things happen. This uncertainty, the numerous myths and the fact that they're essential has brought a bonanza for health-food shops. I wish them well, but the truth is that a balanced diet will contain sufficient vitamins in the same way that it will include enough of everything else. But here are a few important details:

Vitamins B and C dissolve in water, and the rest don't. That means that while you can store most vitamins, you have to have a daily intake of B and C. You'll flush any excess away (it is, incidentally, possible to overstore other vitamins and suffer from vitaminosis, but you'd really have to overdo vitamin supplements to manage it). Vitamin B helps you extract energy from food; vitamin C is part of the repair process. Of the two, vitamin C is the more difficult, because it dissolves in water and breaks down in heat. That means you lose a lot by boiling food, although a healthy diet compromises by having a handsome helping of boiled potatoes and vegetables like cabbage, although neither should be over-cooked. Fresh oranges, blackcurrant, rosehip syrup and parsley are also very strong in vitamin C, whereas apples are poor.

Vitamin B is more difficult to understand. For a start there are many different sorts. The first, B_1, is most closely connected to energy. Australian doctors looked at a collection of athletes and decided they should all be taking more B_1, or *thiamine*, as it's known.

It takes 0.4mg of thiamine to handle 1,000 calories of food, so if you're not especially active and you're using 2,500 calories a day, you'll need 1mg of thiamine to process it. Once you're training and using 4,000 calories, you'll need half as much again (1.6mg) and, if you're riding stage races, very much more. Luckily thiamine is a common vitamin. You get it in liver, bread, cod's roe, bacon, pork, ham, and much else besides. If you're really concerned, you can use B-complex tablets, knowing that any overdose will be flushed away.

For a while the most fashionable B in sport was B_{12}, and there was a trend to inject it in huge doses, even though all you need is a minute amount to prevent pernicious anaemia. It was particularly popular among continental professionals, although it didn't persuade Dr Travers: 'There is no reliable evidence that B_{12} has any effect on human performance, and certainly none that is necessary for normal health, provided that a normal, balanced diet is given.

'I think that one can really discount the slender evidence from the world of professional cycling, since their dietary and drug intake has no rational basis at all. In the world of amateur cycling a much more sane approach is developing.

'I am afraid that there is no evidence to suggest that injections of B_{12} would help athletes in any way at all, provided that they were taking a normal balanced diet.'

The other vitamins are all essential, but you need them in tiny quantities and you'll get them, as you'll have gathered by now, in a normal, balanced diet. Take a multi-vitamin tablet each day if it makes you worry less, but never pig yourself on them because, even if there's no medical disadvantage, you'll get to rely on them psychologically and kid yourself into going slower when you can't get supplies.

Fat

Fat is a wonderful source of energy – it packs more than 4,000 calories to the pound and it contains vitamins A, D, E and K. The problem with fat is that it's a secondary source which comes into use only when sugar has been depleted. In the meantime, the fat is stored under the skin as flab.

It's fat that gives much food its taste – which is why so many nice things seem to be fattening. Enjoy the taste in an undisciplined way and you have to pay the price – it takes 3,500 calories of effort to lose a pound of body weight.

Don't avoid fat completely, because you can use it. But remember two things: that it takes longer to digest fatty food, and that the best riders have among the lowest body fat – 2½ per cent for men, compared to the national average of 15 per cent, or around 12 per cent for women competitors, who have less muscle bulk. The average for all sports is 7.5 per cent for men and 12 per cent for women.

Think about what you eat, and go for boiled potatoes rather than chips, poached eggs rather than fried, sandwiches rather than hamburgers.

Fluid

Everything I've discussed so far has nutritional value. Water doesn't. Water is nothing but water, yet it makes up three-quarters of your body, and your fluid level has to fall only a little and you're in trouble. You can survive without food for months, as hunger strikers have proved, but you'd last only days without water.

Water cools the body, lubricates it and makes your digestion work. It keeps your blood flowing. It was dehydration which made Jim Peters collapse yards from the end of the Commonwealth Games marathon in Vancouver. Dehydration also contributed to Tom Simpson's death during the Tour de France.

Coaches used to tell riders to drink as little as possible because the water would fill the stomach and discourage them from eating the solid food that would bring energy. That's nonsense, of course. In fact you need fluid to digest that food. If you don't believe that drinking a lot will have no effect, try it and see. Drink as much as you can manage and go for a fast ride. At worst, you'll feel a slopping sensation and, before too long, an urge to find a bush. That apart, it will never make you go slower or less far. And that's with more fluid than you'd ever drink in a race.

Your feeling for drink and food is automatic, controlled by the brain following instructions from the nerves. So drink when you feel thirsty, which will be frequently during a race, as that's how you're disposing of the body fluid in the first place.

Of course, there's a balance between how much you drink and the inconvenience of drinking it. Just seconds may govern whether you win or lose a '10' or a '25', and you may lose those seconds in grasping for a drinking bottle. But the relative time lost decreases as the distance increases, and so does the need for drink, so there's no doubt you should drink in a '50', or a 50-mile road race. What you lose will be more than made up by keeping off dehydration.

Drink moderately and don't guzzle. The trick, as with eating, is to keep the body in balance and not to overload it suddenly. If you wait too long before drinking, you'll want to guzzle half a bottle at one go.

Flavour the drink if you wish, but don't over-sweeten it – the sudden sweetness will be neutralized by insulin. Many riders are pleased with commercial preparations such as Gatorade which are on sale from time to time, but most in my experience settle for nothing more elaborate than simple orange squash.

And a last warning: do remember what's in the bottle, or check its contents if you're handed one. There was a 12-hour on the south coast once in which a rider suffering in the mid-day heat grabbed a bottle from a helper and tipped it over himself. It was full of sticky Ribena.

Drugs

Some years ago, a boffin was explaining what were then new approaches to training – the techniques we now take more or less for granted. He had just got into his explanation when a brusque voice called from the back: 'Never mind that – just tell us what drugs we can give our riders to make them go faster.'

There was a silence.

I think – I hope – that attitudes like that have now gone. Dope taking is still about – riders still get nabbed in the Milk Race, the Tour de France and, abroad, in much smaller races. But the insanity of the 1960s and 1970s, when riders died from what they took, has passed. Cycling in Britain is as clean as any sport is likely to be, but it does still go on.

One day you'll come into contact with it, so perhaps I'd better explain.

There are two groups of drugs which affect cycling. The first and more prevalent is the speed group – amphetamine, benzedrine and the rest. They're sold under many commercial names, but they all work on the brain. They give you a buzzing sensation and persuade you that everything you do is better than it is. Sadly, far from being better, it is sometimes (although not always) worse.

For a while, the obsession and concentration they produce might make you faster. Might. The trouble is that drugs unbalance the body so, if you've got everything honed to the balance of fitness, you can't make one part better (whether it's your concentration, your breathing or whatever else) without putting everything else out of kilter. So, even if there *are* better results, they become erratic. Then there's the temptation to take more, because amphetamines are basically not unpleasant to take and persuade you that things are rather better than they are – hence the nickname 'mother's little helper' when doctors prescribed them as pick-me-ups.

Dr Pierre Dumas, the doctor who tried so hard to restrict doping in the Tour de

France, tells of extreme cases that a coach told him about: '... an over-excited competitor who at the finish of a race runs wild in a manner that his defeat does not entirely justify. Or the winner who doesn't realize until several hours after his victory that he has won ...

'I have also seen slobbering cyclists on the roadside, their mouths foaming. Ill-tempered, they kick their bikes to smash them, making disordered gesticulations. Another hits his head with a bottle of mineral water that he's just been given. Yet another throws himself at the barrier and breaks it.

'This would be comical if it weren't so important and pitiable. What can be said of a rider who, in a straight line and on a road 20 metres wide, leaves the road and crashes into a barrier ... and this only a short while after putting his hand into his pocket for a *petit bidon*?'

Continued use can cause severe mental problems.

The second group are the steroids, which build or repair muscle. On a bike, there's no advantage to be had from the big bulk of a shot-putter or hammer-thrower, so steroid-type drugs came into cycling more for recuperation purposes. You'd be able to ride again more quickly, some people reckoned, if you could recover faster, so steroids became good news for stage-race riders and anybody else racing day after day. They also had the advantage that for many years they couldn't be detected in drug tests. That changed in the 1970s, with the world championships in West Germany.

Steroids were used first to build up severely underdeveloped hospital patients. Then they spread to Californian beachboys and from there into sport, with a hefty push from a doctor who recommended them, only to regret and recant some years later when he saw the side-effects produced by the doses that athletes were taking. In 1987 came the first post-mortem in Britain at which an athlete was stated categorically to have died from steroid abuse.

The range of drugs is wide. Some riders found that cortisone would also give the kick of speed they had been denied in amphetamine. Cortisone repairs injuries, so it both stimulated and helped recovery.

Many people have tried to design a new bike, but something really new seems impossible. This weird contraption, with its double gearing, was made for John Howard's attack on the world speed record – around 130mph.

Not as odd as John Howard's mount, but still a sloping top tube, L-shaped cranks and inverted and sawn-off handlebars. How much difference it makes is debatable, but it takes a good man to beat Ian Cammish in a time trial.

The greatest wind resistance comes from the spoke, so the craze for getting the last fraction of speed now includes disc wheels in time trials. However disc wheels are very expensive and many ordinary riders would like to see them banned in Britain.

To this day the subject is still not fully understood. What happened, though, is that riders would acquire a strange puffiness, others couldn't recover from minor injuries (high doses of cortisone presumably making the body immune), and some were quite frank in saying that it had ruined their careers. Bernard Thévenet, who had become the darling of France by winning the Tour twice after long domination by Eddy Merckx, told Pierre Chany of *France-Vélo*: 'I have been doped with cortisone for three years, and you can see the result today: I can scarcely ride a bike.'

Sermons aren't called for, just straight advice: steer clear.

7 ON THE DAY . . .

The best riders don't turn up without shoes. They don't send their entries too late. And I can tell you, from experience as a race organizer, that they don't leave things off their entry forms. It's not coincidence, any more than it's coincidence that good riders don't fluff gear changes, don't have things fall off their bikes, don't . . . well, you can complete the list.

What happens on the day is a culmination of everything you've done so far. If you've been haphazard about training, then you'll be haphazard about everything else. There's no shame in being beaten by people better than yourself – somebody has to win – but it's ridiculous to beat yourself.

Organization

Organization starts long before the season. It starts when you work out your aims and ambitions. And it continues right up to the time you get back from your race.

It's easier and more convivial to race in a team. That might be important in road races, where organizers often give precedence to team entries; in time trials it's not essential, but time trialling can be lonely, and company will give you support on a cold, bleak morning. Team-mates can also share the driving.

Try to race with the same riders all season. Choose people as keen and reliable as you are, people of comparable ability. Three is an ideal number, because being four means that one will end up as a reserve in road races or possibly not be accepted for time trials.

Meet at the start of the season and decide what sort of events you want to ride, when your season will start and end, and what objectives each of you wants to achieve. It doesn't matter whether one would rather win the division road race and someone else the club '25' championship so long as the main thrust will be similar. You'd be very lucky if you could ride the same races all year.

Few races are close to home, so decide what you'll do about transport and how you'll share the cost. Choose who will send off entries – much better, this, than each of you sending his own. Whoever looks after race entries should be on the phone and accessible, because race organizers send start sheets for the whole team to just one rider. Enclose a note with your entries to say who this rider should be, otherwise you'll be a long time wondering whether your entries have been accepted.

Give this rider the option of entering you for another race at short notice if your entries are returned. Trust his judgement, because too much time debating the matter might mean not getting a ride in anything that weekend.

Some clubs have a road race or time trial secretary to do the job. I don't want to undermine valuable unpaid officials, but I suggest that you look after your own entries as a team unless you're absolutely sure they'll be sent and organized impeccably. Make it plain you want to ride as a trio.

The three of you don't have to train together, although you'll need to meet at least monthly to decide which races to ride, to make travel arrangements and to pay your entry fees. You main races should have been settled at the start of the year, when the race handbooks appear.

You should complete your own entry forms and sign them. Your team 'secretary' should address envelopes in advance and write the date of posting on each, beneath where the stamp will go. Remember, the posting date at the moment is more important than the race date. Write the name of the race on the envelope as well and you can see from the envelopes you've got left whether you've sent your forms or not.

If you're riding a time trial, enclose a note stating that you will be travelling together and asking for starts reasonably near each other. Otherwise someone has to hang around for two hours, probably in the cold. The organizer might oblige, or he might not, but you have nothing to lose. Similarly, if you've got some distance to travel on the morning, you can ask for a late start.

Keep a record of all your performances. This should be part of your training diary, anyway, but you'll need almost a computer account of your year to fill in a time trial entry form accurately.

On the Day

Get to the start at least an hour before you start. The only exception is a very early start in a time trial. The hour's margin gives you leeway if something goes wrong on the journey; if you arrive early, it gives you a chance to drive a lap of a road race circuit or up to 25 miles of a time trial course – useful for presence of mind. It's essential to see the finish of a road race, and the preceding five miles.

Travel in your race clothing, wearing a tracksuit (a neat, clean one, and not the one that you train in.) Always wear more than one jersey in a road race or team time trial – if you fall off, the top jersey will slide on the second one, ripping in the process but protecting your skin. This is a mistake I made in my first road race, at Crystal Palace more than twenty years ago, and I've still got scars from the occasion.

Keep plenty of ventilation running through the car, and if it's a long journey, take turns sitting in the back. Get out of the car as soon as you arrive, get plenty of fresh air, and get all the formalities done straight away. Collect your race number at a time trial; get your bike checked and sign in at a road race. If you can afford it, have

Specialized bike racks are elaborate and costly. If you can, collapse your bike and put it in the boot. If not, you have a choice between up-ending it on an ordinary roofrack or buying a junior version of this team rack.

Get to your mark in a time trial only after you've checked who has started ahead of you and who will be following; don't waste time queueing for your turn – ride gently in the road, wait for the guy ahead to start, then report to the timekeeper. Make sure you're strapped in, that your cranks are diagonal for greatest starting effort.

Dernys are worn-out motorbikes – their smoothness makes them good for pacing races, for warming up on the track and even for limited types of training.

a spare set of wheels with tyres pumped ready hard, just in case you puncture with only minutes to spare.

Make sure your watch shows the right time; in a time trial, check it against the timekeeper – don't bother him, just check the time at which he sends off other riders. Now put your car keys where your team-mates can find them. Don't carry them around with you, not only because it irritates your mates but because they're painful to fall on.

Now warm up. Exercise makes you warmer, both inside and on the surface. Ride briskly for between fifteen and thirty minutes, easing off fifteen minutes before the race and stopping ten minutes before the off. If you put your tracksuit bottoms on, the extra warmth in your muscles will last half an hour, and if you don't go too hard in the warm-up, you won't have knocked much off your energy potential.

From time to time you hear of research that claims a warm-up isn't essential. The claims don't come from the performers themselves, so I rest my case on what an old boss of mine, Mike Daniell, had to say: 'Experts at Loughborough have said that there is no physiological reason to warm up at all. My own view is that if they spent just a fraction of the time they give to making these dogmatic statements in getting on with the job of going as fast between points A and B on a bike as they possibly could, we should get nearer to the truth.

'For "25"s in my experience, a warm-up of at least eight miles is essential for the mature riders.'

Don't run around before the start. Don't expend nervous energy. Sort out each job one at a time, get helpers to do whatever they can, and forget the job once you've done it. So many riders waste energy fretting over their bikes, putting their bags down in the wrong place, jumping up and down and laughing with friends. Concentrate on what you're doing – just involve yourself with your team-mates and your coach, so that you can keep up the adrenalin flow.

Get to the line early in a road race. The shorter the race, the more important it is to get in the front row at the start. It's essential at a schoolboy circuit race. Take a place in the middle of the line because officials sometimes move riders on the edge into the second row. Press your quick-release lever into a position where your rear wheel can't be slackened by an accidental touch from someone else's front tyre.

Just before you start in a time trial, ride to where the numbers are issued and see whether the few riders ahead have turned up and whether there are any gaps behind you. You can't be sure of what's happening among later starters, but it'll give you an idea. Most important is to know whether your minute-man and your two-minute man have started, because it will be from them and what you know about them that you will judge your own performance in the opening miles.

You can get disillusioned, failing to catch your minute man, only to find well into the race that the next man is a full four minutes ahead of you.

Circle gently before a time trial and get to the line with fifty seconds to go. That'll give you time to get settled but not so long that you'll get demotivated. Steady your breathing without taking unnecessarily deep breaths (which can upset the balance of oxygen and carbon dioxide); concentrate hard on the road ahead and try to blot out everything else from your mind except the voice of the timekeeper. Throw yourself forward on the word 'go' and get your cruising to its maximum as quickly as you can, without costly sprinting which would exaggerate your oxygen debt.

Time Trialling

Time trialling up to 25 and possibly 50 miles is a skill (and endurance) sport. You probably found this out when you started racing. Most riders improve between their first and second '25' without worthwhile training in between. They simply come to grips with the distance.

Your training will give you that appreciation of distance, stamina and speed, especially if you've managed to use a cyclo-computer to work out split times for each five miles. You can then see whether you start or finish too slowly. You can also see whether your training needs to shift towards stamina or speed.

Concentration is essential. Keep gunning for your minute man without becoming obsessive; don't look over your shoulder for whoever might be coming up. Don't try to stay away if you're being caught, and don't tussle with the man who catches you – apart from breaking your concentration, it also risks taking you into oxygen debt, with the longer recovery time that that involves. And if he weren't better than you in the first place, he wouldn't have caught you.

Pick the best line in the road. Nothing breaks your concentration more than a run of potholes. Concentrate on rolling your gear, using the shoeplates and toeclips as well as the downthrust. Keep down out of the wind – air and wind resistance

All-out start in a time trial. The timekeeper will count you down with five seconds to go; the pusher-off will hold you up, rock you back and forth and then shove you up the road. Concentration is everything at this point; absolute obsession like Dave Lloyd's can get you to your ultimate cruising speed much faster.

increases disproportionately with your speed; and work on not rolling your body – it wastes energy. Don't struggle with a gear, but don't change down too quickly. Your ideal block should have one-tooth gaps.

Take the fastest line whenever you can. The roads aren't closed, but you can smooth off corners where it's safe. Don't stop pedalling until the last moment – the idea is to keep the speed constant, so try not to freewheel and avoid sprinting out of corners. Don't save yourself for harder sections.

Remember that everybody feels stuffed during some stage of the race, as Mike Daniell well recalls: 'No part of a race can be easy. Even when you are going downhill with the wind you must still remember to make it hurt. If you don't, you will have lost valuable seconds to someone with greater courage.

'Never lose heart on the hard stretches. Everyone will have a dose of the creeps there, tell yourself, and smash away that bit harder; never sit up. And remember that the Road Time Trials Council measurers define routes as the shortest way they can legitimately be ridden. There are no prizes for riders doing the best "26" or "51".'

A lot of riders wonder whether they should sprint for the line, but ideally the question shouldn't arise. Perfect pace judgement would get you there without the energy to sprint but also without your being on your last legs. In practice, of course, it's impossible to judge it that finely, in which case there's no harm in sprinting. The advantage is probably only psychological, anyway, because you can sustain oxygen debt only so long, and the difference in speed over a few hundred yards is going to make precious little difference. To try sprinting from further out would only put you into oxygen debt recovery, anyway. If you feel you can ride faster over the last two miles than you did in the preceding two miles, it's your pace judgement that's failed.

That judgement becomes more difficult with distances over 50 miles. I suggest you have at least a mental schedule for a '100', and you might even want a written note on the inside of one arm or stuck to your handlebar extension. It takes experience to work out that schedule, and in the event it's difficult to know what you can do about it, anyway. If you're running behind, you presumably can't step up the

Bigger road races have service cars. Check which side they are travelling if the road is closed (official cars go one side, service cars the other). Raise your arm, pull over and drop back through the bunch.

Stay on the bike if it's a front wheel puncture – it's quicker for the mechanic. For a rear wheel, put the gear into top on the small ring and take out the wheel if the mechanic doesn't arrive immediately.

speed too much unless you've been lagging a bit previously; and if you're ahead of schedule, the last thing to do is ease up. Still, it's a psychological support, especially when you're up on schedule, and it's always good to know how much you've got in hand in case things go wrong later.

Road Racing

Norman Sheil reckoned you could divide a road race field into four. There were those who were there to win and actually expected to win; there were those who could very well win with a bit of luck and expected to be in at the kill; there were those who'd get to the finish provided they didn't over-stretch themselves; and there were a happy little bunch who were secretly pleased to get shot off at half distance so they could settle down to race among themselves.

I reckon that's true in all but the very best races, and even in those you'll find all but the last category.

It stands to reason that the winner, in the end, will be the bloke at the front. Therefore you too should aim to stay in the first quarter of the field. Apart from

Let the mechanic get on with the job; do as he asks because it will get you back on the road more quickly. As soon as the wheel is in place, jump back aboard. The mechanic will push you while you find your toe clips; after that it's up to you.

Of course, when you get really good you get attention on the move – a kind of vroom service.

letting you see all the attacks, it means there's less chance of being knocked off by anyone else. And it also means, if you're a dodgy climber, that you can slip back more before you vanish out the back.

Staying in the first quarter isn't as hard as it sounds on conventional courses because many riders – those who don't want to play too active a role, so that they can be sure of getting to the finish – prefer to ride further back. The front doesn't go any faster than the back, but the whiplash effect on corners is much less marked at the front, so you might just as well ride there for as long as you can. A good reason, too, to accelerate hard out of corners: it makes life really tough for anybody sitting in at the back and waiting for the sprint.

If the course suddenly narrows, of course, you'll have to fight to hold your place. There'll suddenly be more riders than space, and those who stay in front are usually there because they're good enough bike handlers to nudge and push. That's pure skill, and you get it from riding in tight bunches in training, from riding cyclo-cross to feel at one with your bike, and from increasing your strength.

You have to do it carefully, of course. Push and shove too hard and you'll both fall down, bringing down everybody in the bunch with you. And dangerous pushing will win you no friends. The good news is that not everybody is willing to try, so just making it plain that you want to be where you want to be can often be enough. Where it isn't enough is when you're riding against Russians or Czechs or a bunch of seasoned professionals who've done it many times before.

Attacking

Good-quality road races are often slightly slower than the best time trial performances – a fact that time trialists point out with glee. The difference is that road races change pace and that, whether the overall speed is slow or fast, it's still the fastest rider who wins. In other words, tactics play a part.

There are several reasons to split the bunch. The simplest is that you may be able to get your team on one side of the split and your main opposition on the other. And once the split has occurred, the leaders have only to match the speed of the chasers

Take corners fast by pedalling as long as you can. If you freewheel, put all your weight on the outside leg and stare down at the inside of the corner. Never look outwards or you'll drift that way. Pedal out of the corner immediately and use your pedalling to bring your bike upright again.
If you corner in a group, ride just outside the wheel ahead.

to stay away. That's a very simple way of looking at it, but it's absolutely true.

On many occasions, a break comes not through an attack but through a difference of ability or an accident. Riders simply split into different sections – another good reason for being at the front. At other times, though, you have to make your own breaks.

An attack is no more than a sudden increase in speed which other riders have to match. Good places to attack are: on corners, in the last quarter of a hill; at the top of a hill where it runs into a steady drag; when an earlier attack has just been caught; when it starts raining; immediately after a crash; straight after a *prime* (intermediate prize).

In long professional races, teams have junior supporting riders, known as *domestiques*, to fend off inconsequential attacks and to launch their own, so as to weaken the opposition. In amateur races, the early attacks can sometimes matter, so there's much more enthusiasm to get into them. It's rare for an early lone break to succeed, but an early split will usually stay away, particularly if, as normally happens with splits, the better riders are in the leading group.

Early breaks are most likely to succeed when it's cold or, better still, when it's cold and wet. Nobody is as keen on racing in the wet, it's easier to see in a break, and the chances are that many riders lying further back in a spray-soaked, grit-riddled bunch won't realize you've broken clear anyway.

Question: if you were here, what could you do if an attack went at the front? Answer: nothing.

It's also worth trying an early attack in the rain simply because it's safer in small numbers – the more riders there are, the more chance someone will fall off and bring you down as well.

Hot weather can also favour a long break, although rarely before half distance. Heat is sapping and, once a break is out of sight, most riders are content to settle down and merely survive. There'll usually be a chase, and it might succeed, but it's less likely that you'll be absorbed by the whole bunch.

Your chance of getting clear increases with the experience of the opposition, particularly early in the race. If this sounds odd, think what happens in your average thirds-and-junior 50-miler. Everybody hares off after every break as if it were kick-and-rush football. The pace flares and then settles to less than 20mph. Then another attack goes.

The result is that most races finish in a bunch sprint. If you neutralize every attack, there's little point in attacking in the first place. All you've done is ruined somebody else's chance without increasing your own, which is a negative attitude.

The first thing I noticed when I got involved with racing in Holland and Belgium is that even junior riders there had realized this. They'd let an attack go and then try to jump across to it, one by one. It would be shattering, trying to bridge 60 or 70 yards, and some wouldn't succeed. But those who did spent a moment recovering and then put their efforts into keeping the break clear. One or two more riders might join, and together they'd have the strength to pull clear. After a while the gap

The only way to attack from a line-out is to go wide and fast. To go close to the line creates too much attention and picks up fellow travellers; going wide, like Ron Kiefel, is an all-or-nothing business that rewards the courageous who can pick their moment.

would be too wide to jump across. That's a much better technique than just making sure nobody at all gets away.

The cheekiest move I've ever seen illustrates this perfectly. It was a stage race in Essex. Ken Matthews was managing a team of riders from Liverpool, of whom two had broken clear and one was left in the chase.

Before long, the break was well clear but then, to the delight of the chasers, they came back in sight. The chase got to within 70 yards but couldn't get nearer. Something was up, and then we saw what. The third Liverpudlian moved to the front of the chase and, with a great sprint, hammered across to his team-mates. He tagged on the back and all three cruised out of sight!

The point at which you attack decides how many can get away with you. The toughest place from which to do it is the front – it is only worthwhile attacking from the very front if you want to close a short gap between you and the riders ahead. One

Good climbing demands a balanced, open style that lets you use your lungs and spreads the stress around the body. Concentrate on pulling back on the bars, using your toe clips and straps, and employing your back muscles.

In the end, you just have to fight the bike. Getting out of the saddle – 'honking' – puts your weight directly on the pedals, but that's not enough. You have to pull up on the brake hoods as you push down with your foot. At the same time, the other foot must be dragging the pedal up with the shoe plate.
The usual fault is to move the body and not the bike; better to keep your body as still as practical.

rider may get away with you if you jump from three or four riders back; you may get a few more if you start about a quarter back and give everybody good warning. It's better to take nobody with you if you want to bridge a short gap, better to take one or two if you're initiating a break.

If you're attacking in the last mile and you want nobody to go with you, attack from well up the field and switch well clear of the riders you're overtaking.

The way to attack on a hill depends how far up the climb you are and how long the climb is. Most riders are so frightened of any climb that they'll struggle in the wheel of anybody who sets a good pace. It's doubtful you'll get away alone but you may get select company if you sit back on the saddle to stretch your legs, put your hands on the flats to straighten your back, and pick a gear that you can turn briskly

Stay at the front as long as you can on a climb. First, you have more chance of controlling the pace to suit yourself; second, there's more space to slip back; third, some idiot won't hold you up by muffing a gear change; fourth, you can attack on the false flat at the top; and fifth, it's safer to be at the front if the hill goes straight into a twisting descent.

all the way to the top. Don't try to accelerate – just keep pressure on right to the top. The size of the break will depend on how well you do it and how long the hill is.

The ideal hill is a mile or more long, fairly narrow so that it's difficult to overtake stragglers, with its gradient lessening at the top. It's at the top that you'll have your greatest problem. Your body will want to rest, but it's here that you've got to get out of the saddle and attack a bit harder. After all, everybody else will want to rest as well.

Jump (sprint) again, but slip on to somebody else's wheel while you recover. One rider I know had this off perfectly; he'd power up the hill with a team-mate on his wheel and his team-mate would return the favour over the top and on to the flat. It worked more often than it failed, and it only had to work once. A great benefit was that it often got rid of sprinters, who tend to be poor climbers.

Bit-and-Bit

Once you're clear, the rules of rivalry go into abeyance. You work for the common good of the leading bunch until you get near the finish. The aim is to stay clear.

Up to 90 per cent of your effort at speed goes into pushing the air aside. Your bulk and your speed are just about enough to create a partial vacuum, or at least an area of shelter, behind you. So a rider immediately behind uses less energy than his pacemaker.

Riding line astern and sharing the effort is known in America as a pace-line and in Britain by the less lovely but more descriptive phrase, bit-and-bit. The two expressions describe the objective and the technique respectively.

A pace-line works best when each rider has his front wheel six to 12 inches behind the rear wheel in front. Talented riders can get closer. The mistake is to over-react to small changes in pace, because the moment you touch your brakes you'll cause havoc behind you and the point of staying togther will be lost.

Get your line started and settled, then start sharing the lead. Probably around 30 seconds will be enough if there are fewer than five of you. Do your stint and, without easing up, swing out to the sheltered side of the group (if there's a slight sidewind).

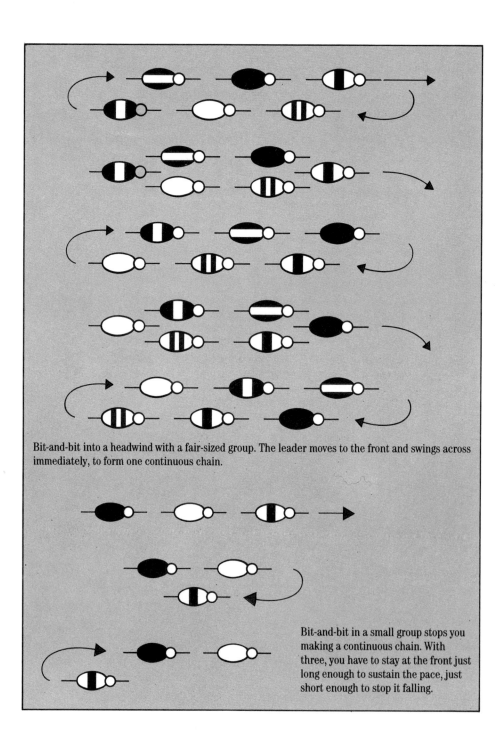

Bit-and-bit into a headwind with a fair-sized group. The leader moves to the front and swings across immediately, to form one continuous chain.

Bit-and-bit in a small group stops you making a continuous chain. With three, you have to stay at the front just long enough to sustain the pace, just short enough to stop it falling.

Most British riders change instinctively to the right, but that will only put you into the wind if the wind comes from that direction, so get used to changing on both sides.

Once you've pulled over, ease slightly and wait for the last rider to catch you. Then slot neatly on to his wheel. You might find this is the time to change down a gear, to rest your legs and to cope with the slight acceleration needed to switch in behind the last rider – to get back on a wheel.

The more riders there are, the shorter your spells on the front. In fact, you'll hardly be there at all if there are eight or nine of you doing it properly – you'll get to the front, pull straight through and swing off. There'll be no gap before the next man swings across in front of you, so you'll be going both up and down the line on back wheels. This steady rotation of riders gives you minimum time in the wind and maximum time in shelter.

It's beautiful to see this being done properly, as it is in team time trials in the Tour de France, but it takes experienced and talented riders.

The problem, as numbers increase, is that they will inevitably include riders who aren't as good at it and the pattern will be disrupted and the effort wasted. There's not much you can do about it, I suppose, other than shout at the offenders!

The time will come when lesser riders get dropped, because bit-and-bit is an intensive effort. Riders in some breaks agree among themselves that they'll reform at the top of hills. On the other hand, a distinctly weak rider is no loss and you might

When the pace gets too high for bit-and-bit, the result is a long snaking line. Only the very best can survive at the front. When it happens in the last miles of a world-class race, it's usually the signal for a series of do-or-die solo attacks.

Compare this with the bit-and-bit diagram: this is the actual thing on the road.

have to go back on your word – it is a race, after all. If you've got a way to go, though, it may be worth nursing a weaker rider, or someone having a rough patch, because he could be stronger later on when you need him. Towards the finish, I'm afraid, luck runs only with the strongest.

Echelons

The wind doesn't always come from the front. It does so only rarely. But it always comes at least partly from the front because there's always the air that you're displacing.

The technique then is to tilt the pace-line across the road. So, if the wind is coming from the left, the leading rider is now firmly on the extreme left of the road, the second man is alongside but a wheel's length back, the third man is a wheel back on the second man, and so on diagonally across the road. Instead of swinging

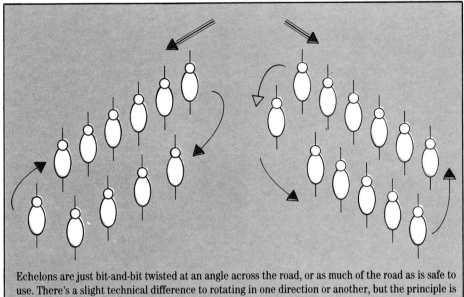

Echelons are just bit-and-bit twisted at an angle across the road, or as much of the road as is safe to use. There's a slight technical difference to rotating in one direction or another, but the principle is the same.

If one echelon is full, quickly shout at other riders to form a second one. Don't hang around trailing behind, which is the usual thing in an inexperienced bunch.

off, the lead man does his stint, eases up and waits for the second man to pass him. He then drifts back along the line of wheels until he reaches the right-hand side. The whole line has then moved to the left to fill the gap that he has left, so there should be a space for him on the right.

In Britain we call it an *echelon*, but it puzzles English speakers who go to France, from where they think we've borrowed the word, to find that the French call it a *bordure*. The Dutch call it a *waaier*, or fan, because that's just what it looks like as riders fan out across the road.

The angle of the echelon depends on the angle of the cross-wind, but it shouldn't ever get wider than 45 degrees to the kerb, because anything less will expose you unduly to air displacement ahead of you.

Sadly, the chances of riding in an echelon are small in Britain. There are several reasons, not least that courses rarely go in the same direction long enough and, even

Coming down the hill you can see an echelon beginning to form as the wind blows from the bottom left of the picture. Now compare this with the diagram of the finished result.

if they did, the roads aren't closed. The effect of an echelon on an approaching motorist is about the same as the approaching motorist on an echelon. The other problem is that echelon riding takes a great deal of skill which British riders, for these reasons, just don't develop. Even Continental professionals, who are much more used to it, often aren't good enough to get in the first echelon and, once there, to stay there. There's only room for one line moving to the left and the other to the right, but even then some riders try to muscle their way in.

If you *can't* get in, instead of starting a long tailback from the last rider, which is what usually happens, it's better to begin another line. Then you can jump from one echelon to the other if you fancy your chances. If you don't get into line number one, you'll still get back into line number two because you're effectively reversing into it.

Disruption

Disruption is a negative tactic applied for some benefit. In other words, you are trying to stop someone else winning rather than trying to win yourself. It can be overdone and it's easy to ruin a race because of it. It's certainly not a technique for schoolboy criteriums and junior road races, where the greatest prize at stake is a couple of training tubs.

There are several reasons to disrupt a race. Most are valid mainly in stage races. Imagine you have got away in a break. Your best rider, who could win overall, is still

Crashes are inevitable, and roads are a good source of tetanus poisoning.
Hospitals are quick to give you an anti-tetanus injection when you arrive. The injections may save your life, but can take the edge off your racing performance for weeks – much better to have a course of injections during the winter.

in the bunch but there with you in the break is a rider every bit as well placed. To work with the break might give the lead to your rival and go against your team-mate, so team loyalty requires you to sacrifice your own chances that day and disrupt the leaders so they don't put your team leader at disadvantage.

They, of course, will have settled into bit-and-bit. Now you have a choice. You could tag along at the back, taking no part in the pace-line but sitting on each back wheel in turn. This will assuredly make you very unpopular, but it also makes it obvious what you're doing. You might also be thought to be saving your own efforts for the finish which, of course, you're quite entitled to do.

Taking no part in the pace-line, though, has little effect on its speed. You can lose a rider in five or six and it makes little difference. So you might as well go through. And this is where bluff comes in. You have to persuade the others that you're riding properly while still achieving some disruption. This isn't easy and there's no guarantee that it'll work.

You could take your turn at the front and just not ride very fast, but that would be obvious and the others will make a point of getting shot of you. There are two other ways, neither of them perfect. The first is to go through at the usual speed but stay there a little longer than you should, so that you start slowing. The other is to accelerate hard when you get to the front and swing over immediately. That knackers you but it also hammers the others as it breaks up the pace.

Dealing with Disruption

The first method is just to ignore it. It's tough work that he's taking on, so, if he thinks you're not even noticing, he might give up. Until he does, just ride round him whenever you can, spreading his effort round the group. But don't get out of the saddle, because that's the extra effort that he wants.

The next stage is to try to drop him, which you might be able to do on a hill.

And then comes positive action, which needs co-operation. You can force him to work. You can take turns in riding off the front, forcing him to respond. You can take turns at taking him off the back. Or, best of all, you can do both.

Taking turns in attacking is straightforward, but it only works properly if there are two team-mates against an outsider. In those circumstances it's not unreasonable for the third man to sit in and do nothing, for his own survival. You can get rid of him by going off up the road alternately. If he responds, the third rider tags on his wheel and does nothing to help. If the chase succeeds, the other team-mate attacks, and so on until one or the other stays away.

You can't do this well in a larger group because everybody else would have to chase as well. But you can take turns taking the culprit off the back. To do this you have to keep the pace fairly high. Then, when the culprit's at the back, the rider just ahead of him eases, forcing the culprit to sprint round. The line settles down again and then the next rider takes him off the back. Eventually he'll crack. Then you either sacrifice the stranded rider or let him outjump the worn-out rider and ease up while he rejoins.

Chasing

Chasing is substantially the same as staying away, except here you have to ride faster than both the bunch and the break. Your incentive is higher, so a well-organized chase often has a good chance. It forms in exactly the same way as the break – the theory being that a small group can chase better than a large one because it's more determined, more organized, and better at careering around narrow, winding lanes.

The lone attack is the epic move. You need a tactician's head, a sprinter's legs, a time-triallist's consistency, and the courage of a pursuiter. A hill attack is a good one because you'll descend faster than the bunch. Lone attacks work where you will soon slip out of sight; where there's rivalry in the bunch; when it's raining; when you can get clear without a lot of fuss (many of your rivals won't even see you go). Lone attacks are suicide on flat courses – where there's nothing to hide you – when there's too far to go, or into a headwind.

But there's a technique. First you want reliable information. There comes a stage when you have to decide whether the chase is worth continuing, whether you're likely to catch the break and when, whether the bunch is making any headway in catching you, and so on.

Two groups of ten, for example, will probably move faster than one of twenty. If the bunch is chasing efficiently, it might be better to close on the break but not catch it. The speed always drops when one group catches another. The break will still be under pressure to stay away, but the chase has the situation under control, and it's in a better position to launch a secondary attack when it does eventually catch the break.

Lone chases make heroes, but there are very few heroes, so you must conclude that lone chases rarely succeed. Still, if nobody else is interested there's a time when it's worth having a go. And there's always the chance that your fugitives won't take you seriously and you'll make ground on them because you can take corners faster and climb better at your own speed.

Lone attacks that succeed earn a place in heaven. They are the classic way of winning and the one way to be remembered. Chancy, but rewarding in direct proportion to the distance you ride alone. Luck might be on your side for two reasons: first, because the other riders will dismiss your effort as hopeless; second because if you *do* get well clear, they may start getting more occupied in sorting out who will come second.

Sprinting

If you can't get away alone, you're going to have to sprint. The racing world is full of people who say they can't sprint but who are actually better at it than they think. There are, though, a few who were born with the right combination of muscle fibres to make them naturally good sprinters. They're big, powerful and very fast.

On the Continent, professional teams have specialist sprinters, and three or four miles before the finish you can see the teams getting into private little pace-lines within the bunch to keep the speed high so that there'll be no late attacks. At the back of each line, riding in protection, will be the star sprinter.

In the last two hundred yards, three team men will belt forwards. They'll be the lead-out man, who'll swing across with a hundred yards to go to give the sprinter a flying start and a gap at the front; the sprinter himself; and the back wheel man, another good sprinter who'll stay on the star's back wheel to stop anybody else using it as a launching pad.

They do it because, although they're all good sprinters, the star is the one who'll win the money that they'll share afterwards.

But there are only a handful of specialist sprinters in any era – probably only one from each country on average. And it follows that not only are there no big teams, amateur or professional, in Britain, but there can't be more than one or two specialist sprinters either. In other words, everybody has much the same chance. Many of the all-rounders who had good sprint finish records, like Eddy Merckx, got them not as good sprinters but because they used their head.

If you're in the last miles and you've still got a known sprinter with you, you have several options. First, you can make the pace erratic by attacking, which is the last thing that sprinters want; second, you can attack on a hill and make the sprinter suffer, because fast-twitch muscles have fewer stayer's fibres; and third, you can box him in at the sprint (although this is a negative tactic which, as well as being chancy and potentially dangerous, will also do no more than stop both you and him winning).

The classic sprinting tactic is to wind up the sprint on somebody else's wheel with about 250 yards to go and then come off the wheel at full speed at 150 yards. You could, of course, refuse to lead out, but it doesn't always work because a sprinter's advantage grows as the distance decreases, so you may save him the need for a lead-out.

Or you could exploit whatever advantage you've got: try a long sprint if you're not much of a galloper – it might not work, but you'd have been beaten in a short sprint, anyway. Lead out the sprint yourself if it's downhill or if you've got a tailwind; the advantage of a back wheel decreases then. Or just take on the sprinter directly, coming off *his* back wheel if you can. Remember, anything's worth trying when you're out-gunned.

Wily Riding

The greatest collection of stars in the world ends up every year in the centre of Paris, riding the Tour de France. With so many stars and so much team organization, logic says that the lesser lights would never stand a chance. And yet the minnows regularly win stages and get their moments of glory. So why?

Well, there are many more minnows than the ones you see winning stages. Those you notice are the shrewd ones who are prepared to take their chances. They are wily, and so can you be.

There's an advantage in being a minnow. You can gain from rivalries between star riders; they won't take you seriously because you've never been a risk in the past; and there's a lot more incentive to get to the top than there is to stay there.

In any road race field, there are only four or five riders who seriously expect to win. That's the case even in national championships where everyone's had to qualify. Of those four, a couple will be preoccupied by each other, one or two might

The joy of winning – in this case Eric Vanderarden in the Tour of Flanders. Building on success is easier than building on failure – tell yourself repeatedly that merely to finish a race is a success and that you fail only by giving up.

be having an off-day, and one might have bad luck. So it's by no means certain that one of them will win. If not them, why not you?

Never let on that you're riding at your limit. It's a good ploy to make others believe you've got plenty in hand. Alf Engers, the first man to take the '25' record under 50 minutes, once said he rode in dark glasses even on dull mornings because they stopped the opposition seeing how much he was suffering. Another rider said he put brand new white tape on his bars for every race because it just stamped 'class' on him, out psyching the opposition. Pete Matthews, the former national road champion, said he put chrome spokes in his *front* wheel, to give him a lift, but put dull ones in his back wheel, to depress those behind. And I remember a lesser light in London–York bluffing better riders so well that he suffered for it in the end – he kept on saying he felt wonderful, humming gently to himself as he rode, that he convinced them he'd thrash them while they suffered. They took turns taking him off the back. It broke him and in the end they agreed they'd been over-hard on him, that he wouldn't have beaten them anyway. But he'd got them pretty worried.

Look for ways to exploit your rivals. Watch for dropping heads, arched backs –

both signs of fatigue. Listen to their breathing. Note how much they're eating and drinking.

Always ride on the sheltered side of the race – if you attack and get caught, make sure your pursuers catch you on the wind side. Ride high on the bars whenever you can, to give your back a rest and to keep an eye on what's happening.

In a time trial, concentrate, concentrate, concentrate. Believe in yourself. Measure what you've done and never what you've failed to do. And never give up.

That way, while only so many people can become world champions, at least you'll know you've ridden to your limit. And there aren't many folk who can say that!

When things get really hard, remember that it's hurting everyone else as well. It's the ability to concentrate through the pain that wins races. Think of anything . . . even count to seven repeatedly . . . do anything but think of the pain.

INDEX